PORTUGAL IN 2023

PORTUGAL IN 2023

Jamie Stewart Jones

Portugal in 2023
Jamie Stewart Jones

© 2024 Jamie Stewart Jones

ISBN: 9798304855709

CPHRC Editorial Services
506-508 Strathmartine Road
Dundee DD39BR
Scotland
stewart@cphrc.co.uk

Contents

Portugal in 2023

Welcome to a meticulously chronicled journey through the tempestuous landscape of Portugal in 2023. This is not a mere recitation of facts or a dry, detached account of events. Instead, consider this a layered exploration, an in-depth investigation into the complex and often contradictory forces that shaped a country during a year of profound uncertainty and rapid transformation. This book looks beyond the surface of the day-to-day, beyond the familiar tropes of sun-drenched beaches and melancholic fado, to reveal a Portugal grappling with fundamental questions about its political structures, economic direction and the very essence of its identity within an increasingly turbulent global order. The year 2023, unveiled through the raw, unfiltered lens of the daily news cycle, was a crucible: intense pressure, startling revelations and profound re-evaluations that left an undeniable mark on the nation.

This is not the Portugal of glossy travel magazines but rather a nation laid bare, its internal mechanisms exposed by the unforgiving glare of the media spotlight. We witness a government initially basking in the deceptive glow of an absolute majority, seemingly untouchable in its mandate. But within months, this illusion of invincibility is shattered, the government brought to its knees by a succession of scandals – each more corrosive and damaging to the public's trust than the last. The year becomes a study in the fragility of power, the caustic nature of unchecked authority and the ever-present tension between promises made and reality delivered. We see how the carefully constructed narratives of stability and progress can crumble under the weight of their contradictions.

The labyrinthine drama surrounding the state-owned airline TAP is not just a singular scandal. It's a potent microcosm, an allegory for the larger political narrative of the year. The story unfolds with the dramatic flair of a high-stakes political thriller: allegations of cronyism and self-serving deals masked by bureaucratic jargon; explosive revelations about secret meetings and backroom negotiations; stolen computers and classified information leading to questions of national security and overreach; and a powerful chief executive dismissed under a dark cloud of "political convenience". Through the TAP saga, we glimpse the often murky, sometimes cynical interplay of power and influence that defines much of the political sphere, exposing individual wrongdoings and a systemic lack of transparency and accountability that eats at the heart of democratic governance.

The year, however, was more than political infighting

and accusations of corruption. It was a year when Portugal confronted deep-seated societal fault lines with a new urgency and brutal honesty despite its seeming stability in Europe. With its exponentially rising rents, the shrinking availability of affordable housing and the displacement of families, the housing crisis rose from a simmering concern into a full-blown national emergency. Mass protests erupted, a desperate cry for change and a powerful indictment of the government's inadequate response, demanding urgent action and forcing the ruling party to confront the raw, human cost of its policies. The demand for housing became a rallying cry for social justice. It exposed the gaping chasm between the state's pronouncements and the lived experiences of many, a testament to the fact that economic growth doesn't necessarily trickle down to all levels of society.

Beyond the housing crisis, the healthcare system was pushed to the brink, highlighting the consequences of underfunding, poor planning and a chronic shortage of doctors and nurses. What emerged was a picture of an institution dependent on the goodwill of a workforce stretched to its limits and a system unable to cope with the demands of an ageing population and a growing health crisis. At the same time, in classrooms across the country, teachers—feeling undervalued, underpaid and ignored—took to the streets to demand better pay and working conditions, a fundamental re-evaluation of their role in society and recognition of the value of their work. All this highlights a country facing the consequences of years of neglect in its social infrastructure.

And looming large was the backdrop of a rapidly changing global context, with the war in Ukraine casting a long shadow over Europe and the world. The conflict became a constant point of reference, a reminder of the fragility of peace and the interconnectedness of global crises. It tested the country's solidarity with its European partners and fuelled a debate about the role of international alliances. The impact of the war, compounded by a surge in inflation and rising interest rates, became a daily concern for ordinary Portuguese. Families felt the squeeze on their wallets as they struggled with increasing mortgage payments, soaring food prices and the constant fear of an uncertain future. The crisis became a lens through which all other challenges were viewed, with concerns mounting about whether the government was truly in touch with the day-to-day struggles of the majority of its citizens.

In these pages, you'll witness not just the grand narratives of the political sphere but also the unfolding dramas in the lives of ordinary Portuguese citizens. The year exposed a crisis of both governance and trust. You'll observe the emergence of new political movements and the re-emergence of old tensions, with parties on the left and right vying for the attention of a disillusioned and fractured electorate. Parties like Chega, with its populist rhetoric, offered narratives that resonated with many voters, underscoring the fragmentation of the political landscape. The year also revealed a society trying to make sense of its place in a world where established norms are constantly being challenged. You'll see the struggle for voice, dignity and a sense of belonging in a nation struggling to reconcile its traditional values with the demands of the modern world.

As you journey through these pages, you will witness moments of unity, solidarity, division, conflict and protest. You'll see how a once seemingly stable political system was rocked by scandal and how a nation was forced to confront some uncomfortable truths about its institutions and identity. But you'll also encounter the remarkable capacity for resilience and adaptability of the Portuguese people, who, despite the challenges, continue to strive for a better future.

The story of 2023 is a story of contrasts and contradictions: of a country with a history of emigration that is now grappling with immigration; of a society that takes pride in its peaceful nature yet struggles with internal social divisions; of a government elected with a mandate for stability, only to be tested by constant turmoil; of a leader once seen as a pillar of moderation, suddenly under fire.

We will delve beyond the immediate headlines to analyse the underlying social, economic and political forces that shaped events. We will explore how the crises of 2023 exposed the fragility of democratic institutions, the complex interplay of power and privilege and the deeply felt anxieties of a people uncertain about their future. Was 2023 an anomaly, a blip on the political radar, or a sign of fundamental shifts in Portuguese society? What lessons can be learned from this tumultuous period as Portugal navigates an increasingly complex and uncertain future? How did the Portuguese people react? What were the underlying tensions at play? How did the political and economic elites influence these events? And what were the real-world consequences for ordinary citizens? These are the questions that will guide us through the chapters that follow.

Throughout the year, the media provided a constant stream of information—a flood of data that requires careful examination to reveal patterns, connections and deeper meanings. This book is an attempt to provide that examination—to sift through the details, to connect the dots and to offer a coherent analysis of a year that tested the very foundations of a nation. We will explore the political theatre, the policy debates and the shifting landscape of public opinion while focusing on real-world consequences for ordinary Portuguese citizens.

The following chapters are not just a chronology of events but an attempt to understand why those events unfolded as they did. We will examine the long-term effects of the financial crisis on Portuguese society, the ongoing struggle to balance fiscal responsibility with the needs of the most vulnerable and the complex dynamics of immigration and integration in an increasingly diverse nation. We will see how the unresolved questions about the country's past continue to haunt its present and how they will undoubtedly shape its future.

We'll examine the unravelling of the government's authority by delving into the scandals that engulfed the ruling party, beginning with the TAP saga and expanding to touch many areas of public life.

We'll analyse how the government's initial attempts to manage the fallout ultimately fueled a growing sense of public distrust and a perception of a system rigged in favour of those in power.

We'll explore the specificities of the TAP affair: the labyrinthine web of compensation, the murky decision-making, the implications of a state-run airline acting like a private company and ultimately, the dismissal of the company's chief executive and chairman.

We'll dissect the events that led to high-profile resignations, the accusations of lying to parliament and the involvement of intelligence agencies, asking key questions about accountability and transparency within the state.

We'll also analyse the impact of the subsequent accusations against Finance Minister Fernando Medina and then Infrastructure Minister João Galamba, which brought the entire government under increasing scrutiny and led to the

Prime Minister's decision to resign when his own name became part of the scandal.

We will also explore the pressing issues beneath the surface of daily life: the housing crisis, healthcare system failures and teachers' concerns over pay and working conditions. We'll analyse the factors contributing to these crises, the government's response and how communities mobilised to demand change. We'll also consider the struggles of individuals and families facing poverty, precarious employment and the soaring cost of living, bringing the raw, human impact of these crises into sharp focus. In doing so, we will also analyse the growing tensions between labour, management and political institutions to evaluate their effectiveness in a modern, technological world.

Turning to the rise of populism and the fragmentation of the left, we explore how the rise of new political forces challenged the traditional political landscape. We will examine the growing support for parties like Chega, tapping into public discontent with the establishment. We will analyse the divisions and tensions within the left as parties like the Left Bloc (BE—Bloco de Esquerda) and Communist Party (PCP—Partido Comunista Portuguesa) sought to distance themselves from the ruling Socialist Party (PS—Partido Socialista) and redefine their role in a changing political environment while also looking at how the newly energised Livre and People-Animals-Nature Party (PAN—Pessoas-Animais-Natureza) sought to represent an alternative left-wing message. We'll also analyse the implications of this fragmentation on the future of Portuguese politics and its overall stability.

We look at the role of President Marcelo Rebelo de Sousa, whose interventions played a crucial role in the events of 2023. We will scrutinise his relationships with the government, criticisms of the system and attempts to reassert his authority as a counterbalance to Prime Minister António Costa and the executive. We will explore how he used his position to shape the national narrative and influence events. We will also evaluate how the political establishment responded to what has been seen by many as an intrusion into political decision-making and ask if the President overstepped the mark, whether some of his actions were more political than presidential and how he has handled growing criticism from both the public and political establishment.

We will draw together the book's key themes to reflect on the long-term impact of the events of 2023 and what they reveal about Portugal and its future. We ask whether the country is on the verge of a significant transformation or simply experiencing a temporary period of disruption. We will also consider the lessons that can be learned from the year and explore the possible paths forward for a country caught between its past and an uncertain future. We'll examine the underlying causes of the discontent and consider what steps, if any, could be taken to rebuild trust in the country's democratic institutions and how these are viewed by an electorate with a history of rejecting traditional power bases.

This book is more than a chronicle of events; it is a search for meaning. It's a call to engagement, an invitation to look beyond the headlines and understand the deeper forces shaping Portugal, a country at a crossroads. You are about to read a story about a nation challenged, a society in transition and a people grappling with the complex demands of the 21st century.

Scandals and resignations

Political scandals, ministerial resignations and escalating public dissatisfaction marked the first month of 2023. The government appeared besieged by controversy, with Prime Minister António Costa struggling to maintain stability and retain public trust.

At the heart of the turmoil lay the ongoing controversy surrounding TAP Air Portugal, the state-owned national airline. The saga began in December with revelations of a €500,000 compensation package paid to Alexandra Reis, a former TAP executive who had subsequently held a government position. This payment, deemed excessive and potentially illegal, ignited public anger and led to the resignation of Infrastructure and Housing Minister Pedro

Nuno Santos, who was responsible for the oversight of TAP.

The fallout from the TAP affair continued to reverberate throughout the month. On 2 January, the Attorney General's Office launched an inquiry into the legality of the compensation paid to Reis. The main opposition Social Democratic Party (PSD—Partido Social Democráta) called for the resignation of Finance Minister Medina, alleging that he was involved in the controversy. Prime Minister Costa admitted Reis had, in all probability, broken the law by accepting an appointment to the board of the Portuguese Air Navigation Company (NAV Portugal) without returning part of the compensation she had received from TAP.

The TAP affair exposed a lack of transparency and accountability within the government and fuelled accusations of cronyism and mismanagement. The ensuing political crisis, characterised by parliamentary debates, calls for resignations and the threat of a no-confidence motion, set the stage for a month of upheaval.

The focus on the government brought about by the TAP scandal triggered a wave of ministerial resignations that further undermined the government's credibility. On 4 January, just hours after her appointment, Secretary of State for Agriculture Carla Alves stepped down due to an ongoing police investigation into undeclared income and potentially corrupt practices. President Rebelo de Sousa played a key role in forcing Alves's resignation, characterising her appointment as a "negative political weight".

Adding to the growing list of departures, Rita Marques, the former Secretary of State for Tourism, faced a potential three-year ban from the public sector for allegedly breaching conflict of interest rules by accepting a position within a company to which she had previously granted benefits while in office. Then Pedro Magalhães Ribeiro, an advisor to Prime Minister Costa, resigned following a conviction for breaching neutrality and impartiality rules during his time as mayor of Cartaxo.

These resignations, stemming from ethical lapses and potential criminal wrongdoing, painted a damning picture of the government. The perception of widespread corruption and a culture of impunity within the ruling PS eroded public trust and intensified calls for accountability.

January also witnessed a series of police investigations and corruption allegations that extended beyond the Prime Minister's immediate circle. On 9 January, the Judicial Police (PJ—Polícia Judiciária) arrested Miguel Reis, the PS mayor of Espinho, on charges of corruption, abuse of power and influence peddling. The investigation, known as Operation Vortex, also implicated Joaquim Pinto Moreira, a former PSD mayor of Espinho who was vice-president of the PSD parliamentary group at the time.

The scope of the investigations widened to encompass other figures within the PS. Finance Minister Medina was scrutinised for contracts awarded during his tenure as mayor of Lisbon, leading to PJ raids on Lisbon City Hall on 23 and 24 January. Paulo Cafôfo, the Secretary of State for Communities, was named as a suspect in an investigation into alleged contract rigging in Madeira.

These investigations highlighted the pervasive nature of corruption allegations within Portuguese politics, affecting both the PS and the PSD. The revelations fuelled public cynicism and raised questions about the political system's integrity.

President Rebelo de Sousa, a figure respected across the political spectrum, emerged as a vocal critic of the government's handling of the January crises. In his New Year's message, he urged Prime Minister Costa to address the political instability and bolster the country's economic resilience. Following the wave of ministerial resignations, the President gave Costa one year to "get his house in order", warning that he would not rule out calling early elections should a credible alternative emerge.

The President's pronouncements signalled a growing concern about the government's direction and ability to govern effectively. His intervention injected a sense of urgency into the political landscape and pressured Prime Minister Costa to restore public confidence.

Facing mounting pressure from the President, the opposition and the public, Prime Minister Costa attempted to regain control of the narrative and stabilise his government. He reshuffled his cabinet, appointing Galamba as Infrastructure Minister and Marina Gonçalves as Housing Minister. He also proposed a new vetting process for ministerial appointments, requiring nominees to complete a detailed questionnaire.

However, the Prime Minister's efforts to restore stability were met with scepticism and resistance. Opposition parties criticised the reshuffle as inadequate and questioned the effectiveness of the proposed vetting process. Tensions between the Prime Minister and the President resurfaced over the appointment process before it was revealed six serving ministers would fail the vetting process, further highlighting the government's vulnerability.

Prime Minister Costa's attempts to regain control of the situation appeared reactive and insufficient to address the underlying issues of accountability and transparency that fuelled the public's discontent.

The political turmoil coincided with growing industrial unrest, adding to the pressure on the government. The education sector witnessed significant disruption, with teachers staging strikes and demonstrations over proposed changes to permanent contracts. Disputes also affected TAP, further complicating the government's management of the airline crisis.

The confluence of political scandals and social unrest created a climate of uncertainty, disillusion and a growing disconnect between the government and the concerns of ordinary citizens, which only added to the sense of crisis. The month's events left the government deeply shaken and its future uncertain. Prime Minister Costa's authority was diminished, public trust in the political system eroded and the looming threat of early elections. The TAP affair, the cascade of ministerial resignations and the widening net of corruption investigations highlighted systemic weaknesses in governance, accountability and ethical standards.

The events undoubtedly marked a turning point in Portuguese politics, signalling a loss of public confidence in the country's leaders and a potential shift in the political landscape.

Growing public dissatisfaction

The turbulent atmosphere continued throughout February with the addition of a deepening housing crisis, escalating political tensions and a series of controversies and scandals that tested the stability of the government.

At the forefront was a burgeoning housing crisis, characterised by soaring house prices, the dwindling availability of rental properties and mounting public frustration. This long-simmering issue reached a tipping point, compelling the government to seek to alleviate the crisis by unveiling a comprehensive package of measures known as the More Housing Programme.

The key components of this programme, launched officially on 16 February, targeted various aspects of the housing market, included: curbing rent increases in new lease agreements; restricting the issue of new short-term rental licences; providing financial assistance with rent and mortgage interest payments; introducing tax incentives to encourage landlords to offer long-term leases; and implementing a compulsory lease regime enabling the state to take administrative possession of vacant properties under specific conditions.

The launch of this programme triggered mixed reactions, with some acknowledging the government's proactive stance and others expressing their doubts about its effectiveness and outlining the potential drawbacks. The compulsory lease scheme ignited a fierce debate, with critics—including former PS ministers—questioning its legality and efficacy. Concerns also arose regarding the potential impact on tourism of the limitations imposed on short-term rental licences.

Opposition parties, notably the PSD and BE, swiftly condemned the programme, arguing it failed to address the fundamental factors driving the housing crisis adequately. PSD leader Luís Montenegro lambasted the programme as "perverse and wrong" and accused Prime Minister Costa of "adopting a communist" approach by proposing such measures.

BE MP Mariana Mortágua echoed these criticisms, asserting the programme would have a negligible impact and would not deter continued protests and insisting people urgently needed affordable housing solutions.

The government's decision to open the More Housing Programme to public consultation until 10 March suggested its willingness to consider revisions. However, uncertainty loomed over the programme's effectiveness and capacity to mitigate the housing crisis and quell public dissatisfaction.

February also witnessed significant shifts in Portugal's political landscape. This included the evolving dynamics between political parties, rising public dissatisfaction with the government and discussions surrounding potential future alliances. The rise of the populist right-wing Chega party continued to be a prominent feature of Portuguese politics. Throughout the month, its leader, André Ventura, repeatedly called for a right-wing coalition to challenge the PS and urged PSD leader Montenegro to join forces with him. However, Montenegro unequivocally rejected this proposal, ruling out any alliance with Chega while he was leader.

Despite Montenegro's steadfast refusal, Ventura persisted in his efforts, accusing the PSD leader of duplicity on immigration by presenting one message to the PSD internally and another to the public. Ventura challenged Montenegro to openly acknowledge the potential for common ground between their parties, highlighting the ongoing tension within the right-wing bloc and the complexities of potential future alliances.

Public dissatisfaction with the government became increasingly palpable as the month progressed. A Eurobarometer survey revealed the Portuguese were among the most disillusioned with the functioning of democracy in Europe, with 75% of respondents feeling their voices were not being heard.

This sentiment was further reinforced by a CESOP poll indicating that 53% of respondents viewed the government's performance negatively. Paradoxically, the same CESOP poll showed that 70% of respondents believed the government should serve its full term. This seemingly contradictory finding suggested a preference for stability despite prevailing dissatisfaction, potentially driven by a reluctance to embrace a perceived untested alternative.

The relationship between the PS and the BE also underwent a notable transformation in February, marked by a shift towards a more critical and confrontational stance from the latter. The BE's coordinator, Catarina Martins, who announced her intention to step down, consistently criticised the government and held it accountable on various issues.

These included the government's handling of TAP, its approach to rent controls and its response to the implementation of the abortion law within the national health service (SNS—Sistema Nacional de Saúde). This shift, coupled with the emergence of Mariana Mortágua as Martins' likely successor, hinted at a potentially more assertive role for the BE in challenging the dominance of the PS on the left.

A series of controversies and scandals further destabilised the political scene. These incidents, often involving allegations of corruption and ethical violations, underscored the persistent need for transparency and accountability within the government. One of the most prominent scandals involved Finance Minister Medina and allegations of impropriety while was mayor of Lisbon.

Reports claimed he had potentially engaged in public procurement violations, rigged contracts in favour of specific companies and possibly even received bribes from contractors. These allegations, driven by an ongoing investigation by the Public Prosecutor, led to opposition parties—particularly Chega—calling for Medina's resignation. While Medina vehemently denied any wrongdoing, the controversy cast a shadow over his position and raised concerns about potential corruption within the government.

The controversy surrounding the substantial compensation paid to former TAP director Alexandra Reis plagued the government. The legitimacy of the €500,000 payout remained under scrutiny, with Medina awaiting a comprehensive assessment from the Inspectorate-General of Finance (IGF—Inspeção-Geral de Finanças) before issuing any public statements.

This ongoing saga highlighted the need for enhanced transparency and accountability in managing state-owned enterprises, emphasising how ethical breaches can erode public trust.

Finally, the publication of the Independent Commission for the Study of Sexual Abuse of Children in the Portuguese Catholic Church report sent shockwaves through the country. The report, which revealed the harrowing extent of abuse within the Church, triggered widespread outrage and demands for immediate action against clerics alleged to have engaged in child sex abuse. The report's findings, which included more than 4,815 validated testimonies of abuse, prompted calls for legislative reforms and a comprehensive response from the Church to address the issue and prevent future occurrences.

More housing, more problems

March witnessed a tumultuous period in Portuguese politics, marked by a series of scandals, policy controversies and economic anxieties. The national airline TAP found itself at the heart of a political storm, while the government's ambitious More Housing Programme sparked widespread criticism and debate. Alongside these issues, the enduring shadow of the child sex abuse scandal within the Catholic Church continued to cast a pall over the nation, raising serious questions about accountability and institutional reform.

The Alexandra Reis affair, which began unfolding in February, reached a boiling point in March, engulfing the government and the national airline TAP in a maelstrom of controversy. At the core of the scandal was the €500,000 compensation payment made to Reis upon her departure from TAP's board, a sum that was later deemed "null and void" by the IGF. The IGF's report not only revealed financial irregularities but also highlighted a concerning lack of transparency and accountability within TAP and the government ministries responsible for overseeing the airline.

The initial shockwaves of the scandal led to the swift dismissal of TAP chief executive officer Christine Ourmières-Widener and chairman Manuel Beja. This move, however, did little to quell the rising tide of criticism, particularly from opposition parties that accused the government of scapegoating TAP executives while shielding those higher up the chain of command.

The IGF's report implicated former Infrastructure Minister Pedro Nuno Santos and his Secretary of State Hugo Mendes, suggesting Santos had bypassed the Finance Ministry and Mendes had failed to inform the Treasury about the compensation agreement. This fuelled demands for accountability and led to the resignation of both Santos and Mendes, while calls for Finance Minister Medina's resignation persisted.

The Reis affair continued to unravel throughout March, revealing further layers of complexity and raising more troubling questions. It emerged that Reis had informed Santos of her intention to step down in December 2021, potentially without demanding compensation. The absence of any documented responses to this email raised suspicions and prompted demands for a parliamentary inquiry. Adding another layer of intrigue, Medina's wife, Stéphanie Sá da Silva, who had previously served as TAP's chief legal officer, was linked to a controversial 2015 aircraft purchase deal, further entangling the Finance Minister in the web of controversy.

The fallout from the TAP scandal extended beyond the political arena, impacting the airline's leadership and its future prospects. Ourmières-Widener vehemently contested her dismissal, threatening legal action and demanding full payment of her salary and potential bonuses. The Court of Auditors also contemplated imposing fines on both Ourmières-Widener and Beja for potential financial infractions, adding to the uncertainty surrounding the airline's future.

Despite the IGF ultimately clearing government ministers of any direct responsibility in the Reis affair, the damage had been done. The TAP saga exposed systemic weaknesses in the governance of state-owned enterprises, highlighting the potential for political interference and the lack of transparency in decision-making processes. The scandal eroded public trust in the government and fuelled anxieties about its competence in managing crucial sectors of the economy. The appointment of Luís Rodrigues, chief executive of regional airline SATA, as the new executive chairman of TAP signalled an attempt to restore stability and move forward.

The government's response to the escalating housing crisis, the More Housing Programme, became another flashpoint for political controversy and public discontent in March. While the programme aimed to address the urgent need for affordable housing through a range of measures, it was met with a barrage of criticism from opposition parties, interest groups and even the President.

The programme's most controversial element was the proposal to compel owners of vacant properties to either rent or sell them to the government. This measure, branded as "coercive leases" by critics, was seen as an infringement on property rights and a potentially ineffective solution to the housing shortage. Other contentious proposals included restricting the issuance of new short-term rental licenses, a move that sparked protests from those involved in the tourism industry, and a mortgage subsidy scheme that was criticised for its limited scope and potential to further inflate housing prices.

President Rebelo de Sousa emerged as a vocal critic of the More Housing Programme, denouncing its key measures as unfeasible and inoperable. He likened the programme to billboard laws—all show and no substance—and even threatened to veto the forced leasing scheme. Opposition parties, from both the left and right, joined the chorus of criticism, accusing the government of overreach, lack of consultation and failing to address the root causes of the housing crisis.

The public response to the More Housing Programme was overwhelmingly negative, with opinion polls revealing a lack of confidence in its effectiveness. Even organisations traditionally aligned with the PS, such as the National Association of Portuguese Municipalities, voiced concerns about the programme's implications for local authorities and its potential to exacerbate existing challenges.

The government's attempts to defend the programme and promise flexibility in its implementation did little to assuage public scepticism. The More Housing Programme became a lightning rod for frustration and anger, highlighting the deep-seated anxieties surrounding the housing crisis and the government's perceived inability to provide effective solutions. The controversy underscored the need for a more comprehensive and collaborative approach to tackling the issue, one that balances the interests of tenants and property owners while ensuring the long-term sustainability of the housing market.

Amidst the political turmoil surrounding TAP and the More Housing Programme, discussions on constitutional reform continued, highlighting fundamental disagreements on issues ranging from the use of metadata to the right to asylum and the potential for introducing life imprisonment.

The controversy surrounding the use of metadata in criminal investigations, which had been simmering since the overturning of convictions in the Tancos case, gained further momentum in March. President Rebelo de Sousa advocated for a constitutional review of the law governing metadata, while Constitutional Court President João Pedro Caupers cautioned against normalising the intrusion into citizens' privacy. Chega's proposal to enshrine the secret service's access to metadata in the Constitution was met with resistance from the PS and PSD, who argued that it wouldn't resolve the underlying issue of its use by law enforcement.

The PS and PSD found common ground on a proposal to reformulate Article 33 of the Constitution concerning the right to asylum, removing the word "political" from the definition of refugee and preventing the extradition of individuals facing threats to their lives or torture. However, the BE's attempt to introduce the term "climate refugee" into the constitutional definition was unsuccessful. A separate Chega proposal to enshrine life imprisonment in the Constitution also failed to gain traction, prompting heated exchanges between Chega and BE MPs.

These debates on constitutional reform underscored the inherent tension between safeguarding individual liberties and ensuring national security, particularly in a rapidly evolving technological landscape. The discussions also emphasized the importance of forging a broad political consensus when considering amendments to the nation's fundamental legal framework.

Beyond the dominant narratives of TAP, housing and

constitutional reform, a number of other significant events shaped the political landscape and public discourse in March 2023.

The Catholic Church continued to grapple with the fallout of the independent commission's report on child sex abuse, which had implicated numerous priests and triggered a national reckoning with the issue. The Church's response, deemed inadequate by many, drew widespread condemnation from across the political spectrum and drove calls for greater accountability. President Rebelo de Sousa urged the Church to adopt a more proactive approach in addressing the scandal, including removing suspected abusers from their positions. The Church's handling of the crisis continued to erode public trust and raised questions about its commitment to protecting vulnerable individuals.

The rising cost of living and soaring inflation remained a pressing concern for many Portuguese citizens, prompting demands for government action. Supermarket profit margins came under scrutiny amid accusations of price gouging, leading to the initiation of criminal proceedings against several retailers for alleged price speculation. The government, facing mounting pressure from opposition parties and public protests, unveiled a €2.5 billion package of measures to mitigate the impact of inflation, including a temporary 0% VAT rate on essential food items, vouchers for low-income families and a 1% salary increase for state employees. However, these measures were met with mixed reactions, with some praising the effort and others criticising their adequacy and questioning their long-term effectiveness.

Political instability, public unease

April saw the continuation of several issues dominating public discourse, including the ongoing controversy surrounding the state-owned airline TAP, the government's response to the housing crisis and the increasingly prominent role of right-wing populism in the political landscape. These interconnected themes played out against a backdrop of economic concerns and a deepening sense of disillusionment among some segments of the population.

The parliamentary inquiry into TAP took centre stage in April, unearthing further evidence of political interference and mismanagement within the airline. The inquiry's revelations fuelled a sustained political crisis, raising questions about government accountability, transparency and the separation of powers. Testimony from key figures, including former TAP executives Ourmières-Widener and Beja, painted a picture of an airline subject to political pressure and lacking clear decision-making processes. Ourmières-Widener portrayed herself as a scapegoat, alleging that her dismissal was politically motivated and lacked justification.

The inquiry brought to light a "secret meeting" between a PS MP, Carlos Pereira, and Ourmières-Widener, which took place on the eve of her parliamentary testimony. This meeting raised concerns about potential attempts to influence her statement and fuelled accusations of undue political interference in the inquiry. The revelation that the PS parliamentary group had met with TAP executives, including Beja before his appearance before parliament added further fuel to the fire.

Opposition parties seized upon these revelations, demanding the resignation of Infrastructure Minister Galamba and calling for a thorough investigation into the government's role in the TAP saga. The IL challenged the government to clarify the nature of the meetings and accused the PS of violating the separation of powers. Adding to the controversy surrounding Galamba, the appointment of his wife to a senior position within the Infrastructure Ministry without official publication in the *Diário da República* raised further questions about potential conflicts of interest and a lack of transparency.

The inquiry also uncovered evidence of political interference in TAP's operations beyond the Reis compensation payment. It emerged that former Infrastructure Secretary of State Mendes had pressured the airline to change a commercial flight carrying President Rebelo de Sousa, which drew criticism from the President and the PS leadership. The inquiry further revealed that the then Infrastructure

Minister Santos had agreed to a bonus for Ourmières-Widener in 2021 despite the company reporting significant financial losses. These revelations contributed to the growing perception of a government entangled in the day-to-day management of a state-owned enterprise, blurring the lines between political expediency and sound corporate governance.

As the inquiry progressed, it became clear the TAP saga was more than just a case of financial mismanagement. It exposed systemic weaknesses in the governance of state-owned enterprises and raised fundamental questions about the relationship between the government and institutions that are supposed to operate independently.

The government's flagship More Housing Programme, launched in February to address the escalating housing crisis, continued to attract criticism throughout April. Despite attempts to defend the programme and offer reassurances, public scepticism persisted, with concerns focused on its potential ineffectiveness and unintended consequences.

Reports highlighting the programme's potential to exacerbate the housing crisis for vulnerable groups fuelled anxieties. The BE criticised the programme for facilitating evictions while failing to address the root causes of high housing prices, calling for rent controls and an end to preferential tax regimes for property funds.

The More Housing Programme became a lightning rod for public frustration, highlighting the government's perceived inability to solve a pressing social issue effectively. Its unveiling coincided with reports of a growing number of people without access to a family doctor and of A&E departments struggling to cope. These compounding crises contributed to a sense of unease and raised questions about the government's capacity to address the needs of ordinary citizens.

Chega, the far-right populist party led by André Ventura, continued its ascent in Portuguese politics, capitalising on public discontent and anxieties surrounding the government's handling of the TAP and housing crises. Ventura's increasingly aggressive rhetoric and Chega's disruptive tactics in parliament further polarised the political landscape. The party's decision to stage protests during the state visit of Brazilian President Lula da Silva highlighted Chega's willingness to exploit symbolic events for political gain.

Ventura's attacks on the political establishment, including President Rebelo de Sousa and his calls for a right-wing alliance, further challenged the traditional dynamics of Portuguese politics. He accused the President of being a "President in name only" for not vetoing the More Housing Programme. He challenged PSD leader Luís Montenegro to "unshackle himself from the President" and embrace a potential right-wing alliance with Chega.

Opinion polls suggested Chega's support remained relatively stable, but its impact on the political landscape extended beyond its polling numbers. The party's rhetoric and tactics contributed to a coarsening of political discourse and a growing sense of polarisation. Its focus on issues like immigration, which it linked to crime despite evidence to the contrary, resonated with a segment of the population and added to the anxieties surrounding national identity and social cohesion.

The political fallout from the TAP scandal and the government's handling of the housing crisis cast a shadow over the PS government, contributing to a sense of instability and raising questions about its future. While Prime Minister Costa insisted on seeing out his mandate and dismissed the possibility of early elections, pressure from the opposition continued to mount.

Opinion polls indicated a tightening race between the PS and the PSD, with Montenegro increasingly positioning himself as a viable alternative to Costa. The PSD leader sought to capitalise on public discontent, accusing the government of "impoverishment" and "rottenness" while highlighting the economic and social challenges facing the country.

The potential for a right-wing alliance between the PSD and Chega emerged as a key factor in the political calculus. Montenegro's insistence that he would never govern with Chega served as an attempt to distance himself from the far-right party while keeping the door open for potential cooperation. The possibility of a PSD-Chega alliance, however, remained a source of concern for many, raising questions about the future direction of Portuguese politics and the potential impact of right-wing populism on the country's democratic institutions.

President Rebelo de Sousa continued to play a prominent role in navigating the political landscape. His public pronouncements and behind-the-scenes manoeuvring aimed to maintain stability while ensuring government accountability. He urged the opposition to offer concrete alternatives rather than simply call for the dissolution of parliament, while simultaneously pressing the government to address the concerns raised by the TAP and housing crises.

The President's decision to veto the law on medically assisted dying, despite his stated support for the principle, demonstrated his willingness to exercise his constitutional powers and challenge the government's agenda. His subsequent call for clarity on specific aspects of the law added further complexity to an already sensitive issue, prompting accusations of delaying tactics from some quarters and highlighting the potential for tension between the executive and legislative branches.

Rebelo de Sousa's approach to the rise of Chega was marked by a combination of caution and condemnation. While critical of the party's disruptive tactics and inflammatory rhetoric, he also recognised the need to address the underlying social and economic anxieties that fuelled its support. His endorsement of President Lula da Silva's state visit, despite Chega's protests, reflected his commitment to defending democratic values and maintaining international relationships. His subsequent criticism of the "excessive attention" given to Chega underscored his concern about the party's growing influence while simultaneously highlighting the need to engage in a broader societal dialogue about the factors driving its rise.

April 2023 was not just a month of political upheaval and institutional crises. Economic concerns remained at the forefront of public discourse, with the cost-of-living crisis continuing to impact households across the country. The government's efforts to mitigate the impact of inflation, including introducing a zero VAT rate on essential foodstuffs, were met with mixed reactions. While some welcomed the measures, others questioned their effectiveness and highlighted the ongoing challenges faced by many families struggling to make ends meet.

The government's Stability Programme, outlining its economic strategy for the coming years, sparked further debate. Opposition parties criticised the programme for its lack of ambition and failure to adequately address health, education and inflation. The PSD rejected the programme, accusing the government of "abdication and exhaustion".

In a positive development for the Portuguese economy, the national railway company CP posted its first-ever profit in 2022. This achievement, however, was overshadowed by the ongoing uncertainty surrounding the location of Lisbon's new airport, with the Independent Technical Commission approving nine strategic options but no clear consensus emerging. The airport project, a significant infrastructure investment with potential economic benefits, remained a source of political contention and public debate.

Political turmoil, economic anxieties and unease about the future marked April. The TAP scandal and opposition to the More Housing Programme exposed deep-seated concerns about government accountability and competence, while the rise of Chega further polarised the political landscape. President Rebelo de Sousa sought to navigate these waters, balancing his role as a guarantor of stability with his commitment to democratic values. The government, facing mounting pressure from the opposition and growing public discontent, struggled to maintain its authority and convince citizens of its ability to address the challenges facing the country.

Galambagate and after

May was yet another turbulent month, marked by a series of scandals and controversies that severely tested the stability of the PS government. The month began with the Galambagate scandal involving Infrastructure Minister João Galamba and his former assistant, Frederico Pinheiro, which quickly escalated into a full-blown institutional crisis, pitting the prime minister against President Marcelo Rebelo de Sousa.

This crisis, coupled with other political developments, including the fallout from the TAP airline inquiry, the debate on constitutional reform and the emergence of a new BE leader, shaped the political landscape in Portugal and raised questions about the government's ability to govern effectively. The Galambagate scandal erupted early in the month, stemming from accusations of ministerial misconduct and the alleged involvement of the Security Intelligence Service (SIS—Serviço de Informações de Segurança) in a matter that many considered to be a police matter. Pinheiro, who was dismissed for "behaviour incompatible with his duties and responsibilities", accused Galamba of instructing him to lie to the parliamentary inquiry into TAP. Pinheiro also allegedly removed computers containing classified information from ministry premises, prompting the involvement of the SIS and the PJ in their recovery. This sequence of events raised concerns about the government's transparency and the potential misuse of state resources, leading to calls for Galamba's resignation from opposition parties like the PSD and BE.

The situation escalated further when President Rebelo de Sousa reportedly told Prime Minister Costa that Galamba was no longer in a position to remain in government, citing the damage caused to the state's credibility. Despite mounting pressure and an offer of resignation from Galamba, Costa stood by his minister, defending the use of the SIS and denying the government's involvement in the alleged theft or subsequent investigation. Costa's refusal to accept Galamba's resignation brought him into open conflict with the President, creating a significant rift between the two highest offices in the country.

This institutional clash dominated headlines for the first half of the month, with the President ultimately deciding against dissolving parliament or dismissing the government "for the sake of stability". However, Rebelo de Sousa warned the government sternly, criticising its "unreliability and lack of respectability" and promising to intervene more closely in its functioning. This unprecedented move by the President underscored the gravity of the situation and placed the Costa government under increased scrutiny.

While the immediate threat of a government collapse receded, the Galambagate scandal continued to cast a shadow over politics throughout the month. Revelations emerged that Galamba allegedly coached former TAP chief executive Ourmières-Widener before her appearance at a parliamentary hearing. Further allegations of misconduct and attempts to cover up evidence emerged during subsequent hearings of the TAP inquiry, particularly in the testimonies of Pinheiro and Galamba's chief of staff, Eugénia Correia. These developments kept the scandal in the public eye and fuelled ongoing criticism of the government's transparency and accountability.

The TAP inquiry became a focal point of political tension, with opposition parties accusing the government of attempting to obstruct its work and shield key figures from scrutiny. The PS, in turn, rejected opposition requests for Prime Minister Costa and other senior figures to testify at the inquiry, arguing that their testimonies were outside the scope of the investigation. This back-and-forth highlighted the partisan divisions surrounding the TAP affair and the challenges of achieving a comprehensive and impartial account of the events that led to the airline's financial woes and subsequent controversies.

The fallout from the Galambagate scandal coincided with other significant political developments in May. Despite his disagreements with the government, President Rebelo de Sousa continued exercising his constitutional powers in supporting and challenging the executive branch. He promulgated several laws, including the controversial legislation decriminalising medically assisted dying, despite his reservations and previous vetoes. He also used his platform to address pressing social and economic issues, such as the rising cost of living and the impact of rising interest rates on families. These actions demonstrated the President's willingness to engage actively in public discourse and hold the government accountable, even within the constraints of his largely ceremonial role.

The month also saw a change in leadership for the BE, with Mariana Mortágua succeeding Catarina Martins as the party's coordinator. Mortágua, known for her sharp criticism of the government and her focus on economic justice, pledged to make BE the third political force in Portugal and provide a strong left-wing alternative to the PS. Her election injected new energy into the party and signalled a potential shift in the dynamics of the left-wing opposition.

Further complicating the political landscape was the Tutti Frutti investigation into alleged corruption in Lisbon City Council, implicating several prominent figures, including Finance Minister Medina and Environment Minister Duarte Cordeiro. This investigation, which has been ongoing for several years, added to the sense of political instability and raised concerns about the integrity of the political system.

Amidst these scandals and controversies, the Portuguese economy showed signs of resilience, with the European Commission revising its growth forecast upward and predicting a decline in the budget deficit. This positive economic outlook provided some respite for the government but highlighted the contrast between the government's financial performance and its perceived political failings.

May 2023 was undoubtedly a challenging month for Portuguese politics. The Galambagate scandal, the TAP inquiry and other controversies exposed weaknesses in governance, strained relations between the President and the prime minister, and fuelled public distrust in political institutions.

A summer of challenges

June was marked by a series of political scandals, economic challenges and growing public dissatisfaction with the PS government. The Galambagate scandal, which erupted in May, continued to cast a long shadow over politics, with revelations about the involvement of the intelligence services and conflicting accounts from government officials further eroding public trust.

The parliamentary inquiry into the troubled state-owned airline TAP unearthed damaging information about the government's management of the company, adding fuel to the fire of public discontent. Economic concerns also loomed large, with rising inflation, the threat of recession, and the government's handling of the cost-of-living crisis all contributing to a sense of unease.

Throughout June, the controversy surrounding Infrastructure Minister Galamba's role in the recovery of a computer from his dismissed assistant, Pinheiro, continued to dominate the news cycle. Galamba's initial account of the events was contradicted by subsequent testimony from other government officials, leading to accusations of dishonesty and a cover-up.

The involvement of the SIS in the recovery of the computer added another layer of complexity to the scandal. Costa denied authorising the SIS's intervention, but his explanation of events clashed with Galamba's testimony to the TAP inquiry. Opposition parties seized upon these inconsistencies, demanding Galamba's resignation and accusing the government of operating by a "tissue of lies".

Public pressure mounted as opinion polls revealed a majority of respondents believed Galamba should resign and that Costa was wrong not to accept his resignation. The scandal also took its toll on the PS's popularity, with the party losing ground to the PSD in voting intentions.

The parliamentary inquiry into TAP, launched in response to a series of controversies surrounding the airline, revealed a pattern of questionable practices and a lack of transparency within the government. The inquiry brought to light the case of former TAP director Reis, who had received €500,000 in compensation when she left the company. Reis reluctantly returned €266,000 of the payment, admitting that it was now considered inappropriate.

Testimony from former ministers further exposed the government's mishandling of the TAP affair. Former Finance Minister Mário Centeno claimed he was unaware of the previous government's plan to use funds for the purchase of new Airbus aircraft to capitalise TAP. Former Infrastructure Minister Santos criticised the 2015 privatisation of the airline and defended his decision not to dismiss TAP's chief executive at the time, placing the blame for her eventual dismissal on current Finance Minister Medina and Galamba.

Former Finance Minister João Leão also contradicted previous statements from other officials, claiming he had not been informed of Reis's departure from TAP and the large compensation she received. These conflicting accounts fuelled the perception of a government mired in confusion and a lack of accountability.

The Galamba affair and the TAP inquiry fuelled growing public dissatisfaction with the Costa government, with many citizens expressing frustration over a perceived lack of transparency and accountability. A poll conducted in June revealed that the overwhelming majority of respondents were dissatisfied with life in the country across various areas, including education, justice, housing, health and the environment.

The government's economic policies also came under fire, with the PSD accusing the government of burdening citizens with excessive taxes while failing to adequately address the cost-of-living crisis. The opposition party pointed to an "unexpected €2.5 billion surplus" in government coffers, suggesting that the government had collected more taxes than necessary.

President Rebelo de Sousa, who had initially adopted a cautious approach to the Galamba scandal, became more vocal in his criticism of the government throughout June. In his Portugal Day speech, he used the metaphor of "cutting off dead branches", which was widely interpreted as a call for Galamba's removal.

Opposition parties seized upon the President's remarks, demanding the resignation of several ministers, including Galamba, Finance Minister Medina, Foreign Minister Cravinho and Agriculture Minister Maria do

Céu Antunes. The President also intervened in the debate over the government's decision to reduce the interest rate on savings certificates, urging banks to increase the interest they pay on deposits. He also threatened to veto parliament's proposals on teachers' careers unless they presented a balanced solution addressing the concerns of the trade unions.

With the 2024 European Parliament elections on the horizon, political parties began positioning themselves for the upcoming campaign. The PS National Commission voted to postpone its National Congress from September 2023 to March 2024, a move widely seen as an attempt to project unity and avoid internal divisions ahead of the elections.

Costa attempted to deflect criticism and shore up his position, calling on the opposition to respect the outcome of the legislative elections and allow his government to function. He also sought to downplay speculation about his potential candidacy for a senior EU position, assuring his party that he was committed to staying in Portugal and seeing out his term as prime minister.

The PSD, meanwhile, intensified its attacks on the government, seeking to capitalise on public discontent and present itself as a viable alternative. PSD leader Luís Montenegro accused the government of mishandling the economy, and reiterated his party's commitment to social democratic principles, ruling out any alliances at the national level with parties promoting racist policies.

As the summer began, Portugal faced a number of pressing challenges. The government's ability to effectively address the economic concerns of its citizens, restore public trust, and navigate the political fallout from the ongoing scandals remained to be seen. The outcome of the 2024

European Parliament elections could hinge on the government's ability to regain the confidence of the electorate.

Government under pressure

July was another month marked by political upheaval, with a struggling national health service and growing economic anxieties. A series of high-profile resignations within the government cast a shadow over Prime Minister Costa's leadership and fuelled criticism from opposition parties. Simultaneously, the country grappled with persistent issues such as inflation, a housing crisis and SNS staff shortages. The month was punctuated by a string of ministerial departures, bringing the total number of resignations during Costa's tenure to a concerning 14 in just 16 months in government.

This perceived instability within the government drew sharp criticism from the opposition, who questioned Costa's ability to maintain a stable and effective cabinet.

The resignation of Defence Secretary Marco Capitão Ferreira on 10 July, amidst allegations of corruption and police searches of his residence, further intensified scrutiny of the government's integrity. The subsequent revelations of potential financial irregularities within the Defence Ministry, including questionable payments authorised during the tenure of former Defence Minister (current Foreign Minister) Cravinho, placed further pressure on the government and led to calls for Cravinho to resign.

The publication of the preliminary report by the TAP Commission of Inquiry on 5 July, examining the controversial circumstances surrounding the departure of former TAP executive Reis, did little to quell the political storm. While the report exonerated key government figures, including Finance Minister Medina and former Infrastructure Minister Santos and his successor Galamba, opposition parties dismissed it as a "whitewash" lacking essential details. This criticism was further amplified by accusations of bias from former TAP chief executive Ourmières-Widener's lawyer, who alleged the Inquiry selectively used evidence to protect the government.

The controversy escalated when Culture Minister Pedro Adão e Silva publicly criticised the Inquiry members, comparing them to characters in a "1960s US procedural B-series drama". This drew strong condemnation from MPs, who demanded a retraction and accused Adão e Silva of disrespecting parliamentary processes.

Beyond political turmoil, economic anxieties weighed heavily on the minds of Portuguese citizens throughout July. The cost-of-living crisis continued unabated, with house prices soaring by more than 50% since 2019. A Catholic University poll revealed the stark reality of these financial pressures, indicating that one in four Portuguese individuals had struggled to afford necessities like food, medication and household expenses in the past year—surpassing those seen during the challenging "troika" period of 2011-15.

Adding to these concerns was the Bank of Portugal's decision to review loan affordability rates to facilitate access to mortgages potentially. While presented as a way to support families struggling with housing costs, the move sparked criticism, particularly from left-wing politicians, who argued that encouraging further debt was not a sustainable solution and could lead to a rise in mortgage defaults.

The pervasiveness of economic anxiety was further highlighted by the findings of another Catholic University poll, which showed that 84% of respondents believed political interference had negatively impacted the management of TAP. This sentiment reflected a broader public distrust in the government's handling of economic matters and contributed to the growing disillusionment.

The ongoing crisis within the SNS remained a significant point of contention throughout July. The month began with the closure of Lisbon's Santa Maria Hospital maternity ward due to staff shortages, forcing expectant mothers to seek care in private facilities. This incident ignited a wave of criticism, with opposition parties accusing the government of neglecting the SNS and failing to address the chronic lack of doctors and resources.

The government's proposal to recruit doctors from Cuba to alleviate the staffing crisis added fuel to the fire. This plan drew concerns about the potential exploitation of Cuban medical professionals. It triggered a broader debate about the ethical implications of relying on foreign healthcare workers to address domestic shortages.

Despite the mounting challenges and public criticism, Costa's PS government maintained a fragile hold on power.

Opinion polls in July showed the PS in a statistical tie with the main opposition party, the PSD, indicating a polarised political landscape with no clear frontrunner. While the government's popularity had undoubtedly taken a hit, calls for early elections were not met with widespread support, and Costa appeared determined to see out his term.

The opposition, however, continued to apply pressure, seeking to capitalise on the government's vulnerabilities. The PSD under Montenegro consistently criticised Costa's administration, highlighting the perceived mismanagement of the economy, healthcare and education. Further fuelling the political tension was a police investigation into alleged financial irregularities within the PSD itself, adding an unexpected twist to the dynamic between the two major parties.

The smaller parties, including Chega, IL and BE, also seized opportunities to critique the government and advocate for their respective agendas. Chega, with its right-wing populist platform, consistently pushed for stricter immigration policies and a tougher stance on crime. At the same time, IL sought to position itself as a liberal alternative focused on economic reforms and individual liberties. The BE, representing the left-wing, criticised the government's economic policies and advocated for more lavish social spending and worker protections.

As July drew to a close, Portugal found itself at a crossroads. The political landscape remained volatile, with the government battling accusations of corruption and struggling to maintain public trust. The economy continued to present significant challenges, with inflation and the housing crisis putting immense strain on citizens. Plagued by staff shortages and underfunding, the SNS faced an uphill battle to provide adequate healthcare.

The Costa government, facing a barrage of criticism

and waning public support, needed to demonstrate decisive action to address the nation's multifaceted challenges. The opposition, emboldened by the government's vulnerabilities, intensified its scrutiny and push for alternative solutions. The Portuguese people, grappling with economic hardship and uncertainty about the future, awaited concrete measures to alleviate their anxieties and restore confidence in the country's leadership.

Pilgrims and politics

August was marked by a series of significant events that captivated the nation's attention and shaped its political discourse. The month began with the highly anticipated World Youth Day festival in Lisbon, attracting more than a million pilgrims and culminating in a visit by Pope Francis. As the religious fervour subsided, the political landscape heated up with controversies surrounding government policies, economic concerns and looming elections.

The beginning of August saw Lisbon transformed into a hub of religious activity as it hosted the World Youth Day festival. While the event brought a sense of spiritual unity and global attention to the capital, it also sparked debate about the close relationship between the state and the

Church, particularly regarding the funding of the festival. The arrival of more than a million pilgrims, nearly tripling Lisbon's population, led to logistical challenges and disruptions, forcing many residents to leave the city temporarily. Critics, including Chega leader Ventura, raised concerns about potential financial irregularities in the event's organisation, demanding scrutiny by the Court of Auditors. Prime Minister Costa, however, defended the festival, emphasising its economic benefits through tourism and increased spending.

Pope Francis' arrival in Lisbon on 3 August marked the pinnacle of the festival, with his pronouncements resonating throughout the country and beyond. His meeting with 13 victims of child sex abuse by priests highlighted the Church's ongoing struggle with this sensitive issue. The Pope's call for change within the Church and his warning to Europe about the refugee crisis and social issues like euthanasia and abortion further amplified his influence on the national conversation. While political leaders from various parties praised the Pope's message on global issues like climate change and youth empowerment, the financial transparency of the event remained a point of contention, with parties like Chega and PAN demanding the government disclose the total cost.

Beyond the religious spectacle, several political developments shaped the month's news cycle. The appointment of a new director for the Strategic Defence Information Service followed the resignation of the previous incumbent amid corruption allegations, highlighting ongoing concerns about transparency and accountability within the government. Further controversies arose when the government approved the felling of more than 1,800 cork oak trees to facilitate a wind farm project, drawing criticism from environmental groups like PAN, which argued for a more sustainable approach to the energy transition.

The political landscape was also stirred by internal party dynamics. The resignation of Paulo Freitas do Amaral from the Popular Party (PP—Partido Popular) and his intention to create a new centrist party signalled dissatisfaction with the party's direction and its perceived abandonment of its core values. Meanwhile, Chega leader Ventura continued to push his agenda, advocating for constitutional changes to allow whole-life sentences for crimes against children and challenging the government's transparency on issues ranging from World Youth Day expenditures to accommodation for police officers during the event. Ventura's assertive approach, coupled with his party's growing popularity among certain demographics, suggested Chega's increasing influence within the political spectrum.

Economic concerns also played a significant role in August. The unemployment rate fell to 6.1% in June, but the growth was largely attributed to precarious employment and part-time contracts, raising questions about the quality and sustainability of job creation. Public sector arrears, while lower than the previous year, still amounted to a significant sum, indicating ongoing financial challenges for the government. The rising cost of living, reflected in issues like soaring student accommodation prices and the lowest minimum wage in seven years, added to the economic anxieties of many Portuguese citizens.

Social issues, too, contributed were a concern. Media reports emerged about 30,000 foreign children enrolling in pre-school and primary schools, underscoring the impact of immigration on the education system. The debate on medically assisted dying and abortion laws, ignited by Pope Francis' criticism, continued to divide public opinion.

Meanwhile, the government announced plans to ensure school textbooks are free from racism and sexism, heralding its commitment to promoting inclusivity and equality in education.

The second half of August was dominated by a wave of wildfires that ravaged various parts of the country, exacerbated by scorching temperatures and strong winds. The fires led to the evacuation of thousands of people, with Odemira in the south being particularly hard hit. The government's initial reluctance to declare a state of alert, despite calls from opposition figures like Ventura, drew criticism for its perceived slow response to the crisis. As the fires raged on, destroying thousands of hectares of land, concerns grew about the long-term environmental and economic impact of these natural disasters. The government eventually committed to assessing the damage and providing support to those affected, but the adequacy and timeliness of its response remained under scrutiny.

As the month drew to a close, the focus shifted towards upcoming political battles. The Madeira Autonomous Region elections, scheduled for September, became a key talking point, with polls suggesting potential gains for Chega and Ventura reiterating his ambition to deny the governing coalition a majority. The Constitutional Court's rejection of Chega's appeal against the annulment of its party convention introduced further uncertainty into the electoral landscape, potentially impacting the validity of its candidates. However, the Madeira District Judicial Court's subsequent approval of Chega's candidates, despite challenges from other parties, kept the party's participation in the elections alive.

Beyond the regional elections, the 2026 Presidential election started garnering attention. Speculation arose around potential candidates, with former PSD leader

Marques Mendes expressing interest in running and Chega's Ventura announcing his party's intention to field a candidate. These early manoeuvres pointed towards a potentially intense and unpredictable race for the presidency.

The month concluded with the PSD's Summer University, a platform for future party leaders to discuss key issues. Former deputy prime minister and ex-leader of the PP Paulo Portas spoke to delegates about the 2026 Presidential elections, advocating a focus on replacing the current government rather than the President in the upcoming elections.

Vetoes to elections

September unfolded as a month marked by heightened political tensions, economic anxieties and a looming sense of uncertainty surrounding the government's ability to address pressing issues. The simmering conflict between Prime Minister Costa and President Rebelo de Sousa, ignited by the President's veto of the government's flagship More Housing Programme, escalated into a public display of discord, further eroding public trust and raising questions about the stability of the ruling PS.

The housing crisis, already a major concern, emerged as a central theme throughout September, exacerbating existing political tensions and fuelling public discontent. The month began with reports of soaring non-controlled rents, prompting Prime Minister Costa to write to European Commission President Ursula von der Leyen, urging her to prioritise housing costs and address the flight of talent. The government's More Housing Programme remained a point of contention between the President and the prime minister. Despite the likelihood of the package passing in Parliament for a second time, effectively overturning the President's veto, the President emphasised that the second part of the law, containing crucial regulatory details, was yet to be presented for his approval. His characterisation of the housing issue as a "race against the clock" added urgency to the debate and underscored the need for swift and decisive action.

The President's continued scrutiny of the housing policy, particularly his pledge to maintain pressure on the government despite constitutional constraints preventing a second veto, cast a veil of uncertainty over the More Housing Programme. Opposition parties seized the opportunity to criticise the government's handling of the crisis. PSD leader Montenegro accused the government of being "completely adrift" and "leading Portugal into a bleak future" on housing, arguing the More Housing Programme would actually reduce housing availability and drive up prices. BE coordinator Mortágua dismissed the dispute between the President and the prime minister as a "palace dispute" and a "distraction" from the urgent need for solutions to the housing crisis. This sentiment was echoed by PP leader Nuno Melo, who criticised the PS for its failure on housing policy.

The European Commission's response to Prime Minister Costa's request for additional support and tools to address the housing crisis further complicated matters. Brussels rejected the idea of shifting responsibility for housing to the EU, advising Lisbon to address its housing problem internally. This rejection placed the onus firmly on the Portuguese government to find effective solutions, amplifying the pressure on Costa and his administration. As the month progressed, the housing crisis continued to dominate the political discourse, with opposition parties consistently challenging the government's policies and demanding more effective measures to alleviate the burden on citizens struggling with rising rents and mortgage payments.

The month also witnessed a marked escalation in the political sparring between Prime Minister Costa and President Rebelo de Sousa, further straining relations between the two highest offices in the country and raising concerns about the erosion of institutional trust. The tense atmosphere surrounding the Council of State meeting on 6 September epitomised this growing discord. Prime Minister Costa's decision to remain silent when invited to speak by the President, particularly his refusal to praise the President's visit to Kyiv and instead reiterate only his government's commitment to Ukraine, created a palpable sense of unease. The President's surprise at Costa's reticence and the media's portrayal of the meeting as tense further highlighted the breakdown in communication and the growing rift between the two leaders.

The fall-out from the Council of State meeting reverberated throughout the following days. Opposition parties, particularly the PSD, seized on Costa's silence as evidence of his disregard for democratic institutions. PSD leader Montenegro accused Costa of "degrading democratic institutions", describing him as "sulking" instead of providing explanations on economic and social issues as expected of the head of government. Montenegro's expression of concern about the "country's impoverishment and institutional degradation" resonated with a public increasingly disillusioned with the political climate.

Prime Minister Costa's response to the President's veto of the More Housing Programme further fuelled the perception of institutional discord. His emphasis on the importance of each state institution respecting the competencies of others and their roles in governing the country was widely interpreted as a veiled criticism of the President's intervention. His assertion that it is important for "everyone to stay in their respective lanes for the state to function effectively" and his self-portrayal as a "doer" rather than a "critic" further exacerbated the tension between the two men.

The ongoing public spat between the President and the prime minister, amplified by media coverage and opposition rhetoric, contributed to a growing sense of unease among the Portuguese public. This erosion of trust in the country's highest institutions, particularly amidst a backdrop of economic anxieties and a persistent housing crisis, cast a shadow over the political landscape and raised concerns about the government's ability to effectively address the challenges facing the nation.

Against the backdrop of a challenging economic environment, characterised by rising inflation, surging mortgage payments and concerns about the impact of the European Central Bank's monetary policy, the government sought to introduce measures aimed at providing relief to citizens while maintaining fiscal responsibility. The announcement of several measures targeted at young people during Prime Minister Costa's speech at the PS Academy in Évora on 7 September signalled the government's awareness of the need to address the economic anxieties of a key demographic. Proposals such as a gradual exemption from paying income tax over the first five years of employment, tax exemptions for young workers during their first year of employment, free public transport passes for those under 23 and various other benefits were designed to ease the financial burden on young people entering the workforce. The extension of the temporary zero VAT rate on essential food products until the end of the year represented another attempt to mitigate the impact of rising living costs on households.

Despite the government's efforts, opposition parties remained critical of the proposed measures, arguing they were insufficient to address the underlying economic challenges. The PSD dismissed the proposals as "poor imitations" of their own ideas, characterising the prime minister as a "follower who copies badly" rather than a true leader. IL leader Rui Rocha described the measures as a "deception" that the youth "will see through", while Chega criticised Costa for offering "palliatives" instead of meaningful solutions. On the left, the PCP argued that the measures would do little to address low wages and precarious employment, while BE coordinator Mortágua accused the government of delaying and minimising repayments to taxpayers without tackling the real issues facing society.

The government's announcement of two new mechanisms designed to stabilise mortgage payments for two years, preventing sudden increases due to rising interest rates and providing households with some financial certainty, further highlighted the focus on mitigating the impact of economic pressures on citizens. These measures, along with Finance Minister Medina's announcement of three additional measures as part of the More Housing Programme, including a 13% interest relief and a 30% discount on Euribor rates in November, underscored the government's commitment to addressing the housing crisis and its economic ramifications.

However, the sustainability of these measures and their long-term effectiveness in tackling the underlying economic challenges remained open to debate. Opposition parties continued to push for more substantial tax cuts and argued that the government's interventions, while providing temporary relief, did not address the structural issues hindering economic growth and prosperity. The balancing act between providing immediate relief to citizens struggling with the rising cost of living and ensuring the long-term health of the economy remained a key challenge for the government as it prepared to unveil the 2024 state budget in October.

The regional elections in Madeira, held on 24 September, offered a glimpse into the evolving political landscape in the country, reflecting national trends and the growing influence of parties outside the traditional two-party system. The PSD-PP coalition, led by Miguel Albuquerque, emerged as the largest group, securing 43.13% of the vote but falling one seat short of an overall majority. The election marked the entry of Chega and IL into the regional parliament, while the PS suffered a significant decline in support, allowing BE and PAN to regain their parliamentary representation.

Despite earlier pronouncements that he would resign should he fail to achieve a majority, Albuquerque swiftly announced his intention to negotiate with IL and PAN to form a government. The willingness of both IL and PAN to engage in talks with Albuquerque, despite previous statements that they would not, highlighted the fluid nature of political alliances. IL leader Rui Rocha's expression of readiness to discuss key issues like tax cuts, healthcare waiting lists, transparency, corruption and political cronyism with Albuquerque signalled a potential shift in the political dynamics of the region.

The PSD's national leadership firmly ruled out any possibility of Albuquerque governing with the support of Chega, highlighting the party's attempts to distance itself from the far-right party. Chega leader Ventura's call for Albuquerque's immediate resignation and his party's refusal to enter into any agreements or alliances further underlined the deep divisions within the right-wing bloc.

The eventual parliamentary agreement between the PSD-PP coalition and PAN, enabling the formation of a government despite the lack of an absolute majority, demonstrated the growing importance of smaller parties in shaping political outcomes. This pact, while criticised by some within both parties, illustrated the potential for cross-ideological collaboration in addressing regional challenges. The agreement's focus on issues like the introduction of a tourist tax, improved rent support and free sterilisation and vaccination of domestic pets highlighted the influence of PAN's policy priorities on the regional agenda.

The Madeira regional elections underscored the fragmentation of the political landscape, the rise of new political forces and the willingness of parties to forge unconventional alliances to achieve their objectives. The results served as a reminder of the dynamic nature of Portuguese politics and the potential for significant shifts in power dynamics as the country navigates a period of economic uncertainty and political discontent.

As September drew to a close, the country found itself at a crossroads, grappling with a multitude of challenges and uncertainties. The public display of discord between the President and the prime minister, fuelled by disagreements over the More Housing Programme and exacerbated by the tense Council of State meeting, raised concerns about the stability of the government and its ability to effectively address pressing issues. The housing crisis continued to cast a long shadow over the political landscape, with opposition parties consistently challenging the government's policies and demanding more robust measures to alleviate the burden on citizens. The economic landscape remained fragile, characterised by rising inflation, surging mortgage payments and the potential impact of the ECB's monetary policy on household finances. The government's attempts to mitigate these pressures through targeted relief measures, while welcomed by some, faced criticism from opposition parties that argued for more substantial tax cuts and structural reforms.

The outcome of the Madeira regional elections, while providing the PSD-PP coalition with a path to continue governing, also highlighted the fragmentation of the political landscape and the rise of new political forces like Chega and IL. The willingness of smaller parties to enter unconventional alliances to achieve their objectives added a layer of complexity to the political dynamics, making future political outcomes more unpredictable.

As Portugal prepared for the 2024 budget announcement in October, the government faced a daunting task: balancing the need to provide relief to citizens struggling with the rising cost of living with the imperative to maintain fiscal responsibility and address the underlying structural issues hindering economic growth.

Budgets and privatisation

Portugal in October was a nation grappling with a multitude of challenges. The month was marked by a persistent crisis in the SNS, fierce debates surrounding the 2024 state budget and the controversial proposed privatisation of the national airline TAP. These issues were further amplified by the looming European Parliament elections, adding another layer of complexity to the already charged political landscape.

One of the most dominant themes throughout October was the deepening crisis engulfing the SNS, with a chronic shortage of doctors forcing many hospitals to close or significantly curtail their emergency services. The gravity of the situation was evident in the widespread refusal of doctors to work overtime beyond the legal limit of 150 hours per week. Carlos Cortes, President of the Order of Physicians, described the situation as "catastrophic" and demanded an urgent meeting with Health Minister Manuel Pizarro to address the crisis. Further compounding the problem was the alarming rate at which doctors were leaving the public health service, with 705 departures in 2023 and a projected 1,200 exits in 2024. This exodus, coupled with the lack of adequate replacements, pushed the service to breaking point, leading to the closure or implementation of "contingency measures" in up to 27 hospital A&E departments by 4 October. Major hospitals in Lisbon and Porto, traditionally considered better staffed, were also affected, indicating the widespread nature of the crisis.

The Doctors in Protest movement, which gained momentum throughout the month, served as a stark reminder of the frustration and "desperation within the health profession". Their refusal to work overtime was not simply a labour dispute; it was a cry for help from a system on the verge of collapse, with experts warning that even the government's planned health service reforms, intended to address systemic issues, would fall short without a concerted effort to recruit and retain doctors.

Unsurprisingly, the opposition parties capitalised on this crisis, leveraging it to criticise the government's handling of the situation. Calls for parliamentary debates to address the chaos in the health service became increasingly frequent, with some even demanding presidential intervention. IL leader Rocha, known for his sharp critiques of the government, directly blamed Prime Minister Costa for the crisis, accusing him of relying on "patchwork solutions" instead of implementing meaningful structural reforms. Chega leader Ventura went further, declaring the health service to be on the brink of collapse and blaming the service's senior management.

Despite the government's insistence that adequate funding had been allocated to the SNS in the 2024 budget, doubts lingered about its commitment and ability to effectively tackle the crisis. The public health service's Executive Director, Fernando Araújo, painted a grim picture, warning of a potentially "dramatic" situation in November if a resolution is not reached between doctors and the government. His proposal to restrict access to hospital A&E departments, allowing only patients referred by doctors or the NHS24 hotline, exacerbated anxieties. Opposition parties seized upon Araújo's statements, accusing him of scaremongering, and questioned President Rebelo de Sousa's decision to promulgate the government's health service bills despite widespread reservations.

The severity of the crisis was underscored by PSD leader Montenegro's decision to seek an urgent meeting with President Rebelo de Sousa to convey his concerns about the state of the public health service. The meeting highlighted the widespread perception that the government was failing to adequately address a problem with far-reaching consequences for Portuguese society.

The unveiling of the 2024 state budget by Finance Minister Medina on 11 October marked a pivotal moment in Portuguese politics, setting the stage for weeks of intense debate and scrutiny. While the budget included some crowd-pleasing measures, such as widespread income tax reductions, increases to pensions and the minimum wage, and even a projected budget surplus of €2.2 billion, it also sparked significant controversy, particularly surrounding the planned increase in the Vehicle Licensing Tax for vehicles registered before 2007.

The budget became a focal point for opposition attacks, with parties across the political spectrum highlighting what they perceived to be its shortcomings. The

PCP and IL, representing the left and right respectively, were quick to dismiss the budget as "propaganda-driven", criticising the overall tax burden and the lack of concrete measures to address the pressing issue of the housing crisis. PSD leader Montenegro adopted a similar line of attack, accusing the government of focusing its efforts on benefiting the wealthy at the expense of the broader population. IL leader Rocha, in his characteristically blunt style, accused the government of "fiscal cruelty", arguing that the vehicle tax increase would disproportionately impact those with fewer resources who are more likely to own older cars.

The budget debate exposed the deep ideological divides within Portuguese politics. The government defended its approach, emphasising the need for fiscal responsibility while simultaneously supporting vulnerable segments of society. Opposition parties, however, painted a different picture, arguing the budget fails to adequately address the real concerns of ordinary citizens. The stage was set for a potentially dramatic parliamentary vote on the budget scheduled for the last day of the month, with the opposition parties vowing to vote against it.

The government's long-held ambition to privatise the national airline TAP encountered significant turbulence in October, culminating in a dramatic veto by President Rebelo de Sousa on 30 October. This unexpected move sent shockwaves through the political landscape and ignited a fierce debate about the government's handling of the privatisation process. Opposition leaders, sensing an opportunity to exploit the government's vulnerability, were quick to condemn the situation. PSD leader Montenegro accused Prime Minister Costa of "deceit and political and financial wrongdoing" in relation to the privatisation and demanded a public apology. Chega leader Ventura echoed these sentiments, criticising the government's "irresponsibility" and calling for further scrutiny of its actions.

To contain the fallout from the presidential veto, Costa used the parliamentary budget debate to address concerns about the TAP privatisation. He insisted that price was not the primary consideration in the sale and offered assurances that the airline would not be sold without guarantees from the buyer that Lisbon would remain its main hub. However, these assurances were met with scepticism from some quarters, with former Infrastructure Minister Santos describing them as a "smokescreen" and calling for greater transparency in the privatisation process.

The TAP saga highlighted the political sensitivity surrounding the fate of the national airline. The government's determination to proceed with privatisation, despite opposition from various stakeholders, fuelled accusations of a lack of transparency and a disregard for public opinion. The presidential veto only intensified these concerns, leaving the future of TAP shrouded in uncertainty.

With the European Parliament elections scheduled for June 2024 drawing closer, the political climate in Portugal became increasingly charged with a dynamic and unpredictable race between the ruling PS and the main opposition PSD both vying for public support. Opinion polls conducted throughout October offered a glimpse into this evolving landscape, showing fluctuating levels of support for both parties. The PSD briefly enjoyed a narrow lead over the PS in some polls, only to see its advantage evaporate in subsequent surveys. The consistent presence of Chega as the third most popular party added another layer of complexity to the electoral equation, with the potential to significantly influence the outcome.

The pre-election period saw both the government and opposition parties actively working to consolidate their positions and appeal to voters. The government sought to highlight its economic achievements, pointing to the budget surplus and income tax reductions as evidence of its sound management. The opposition parties, however, focused their critiques on issues that resonate with public anxieties, such as the healthcare crisis, the rising cost of living and perceived government mismanagement of EU funds.

The European Parliament elections represented a crucial opportunity for both the government and the opposition to gauge public sentiment and assess their electoral strength, with the outcome of these elections expected to have significant implications for the 2026 general election and shape the political landscape for years to come.

The events of October 2023 offer a compelling snapshot of Portugal at a crossroads. The nation was grappling with a confluence of challenges, including a healthcare system in crisis, a controversial state budget and a contentious privatisation process. The looming European Parliament elections only added to the intensity of the political atmosphere, as parties positioned themselves for a pivotal electoral battle.

Fall of the government

A tumultuous month marked by a deepening healthcare crisis, contentious budget negotiations and the sudden resignation of Prime Minister Costa. These events, interwoven with the upcoming PS leadership election and the looming general election in March 2024, painted a picture of a nation grappling with uncertainty and the potential for significant political change.

The crisis gripping the SNS continued and was characterised by a severe shortage of doctors, prompting widespread closures of A&E departments and the cancellation of operations. The ongoing disagreement between the Health Ministry and doctors' unions over salary increases led to the refusal of many doctors to work overtime, further exacerbating the strain on an already stretched system. The dire consequences of this impasse were palpable, with reports of intensive care beds being shut down and patients facing lengthy waiting times for essential medical care. The crisis extended beyond major cities, impacting hospitals across the country, signifying the systemic nature of the problem.

This was a healthcare system that appeared to be teetering on the brink of collapse, with experts warning of dire consequences should a solution not be reached swiftly. The Doctors in Protest movement, indicative of the growing frustration and disillusionment within the medical profession, served as a potent symbol of the crisis. The government's proposed health service reforms, intended to address the systemic issues plaguing the SNS, appeared insufficient in the face of the acute shortage of doctors and the escalating demands on the system.

The SNS crisis became a focal point for opposition parties, who relentlessly criticised the government's handling of the situation. They argued the government's response was inadequate and reactive, lacking a coherent strategy to address the root causes of the crisis. Calls for increased investment in the SNS, better working conditions for doctors and a comprehensive plan to recruit and retain healthcare professionals became increasingly strident. The government's defence, highlighting increased funding for the SNS in the 2024 budget, was met with disbelief as the crisis continued to unfold unabated.

The presentation of the 2024 state budget by Finance Minister Medina marked a turning point in the political landscape, triggering a wave of controversy and intensifying tensions between the government and the opposition. The budget, while including provisions for income tax reductions and increases to pensions and the minimum wage, also proposed a contentious hike in road tax for older vehicles. This measure sparked widespread public outrage, with protests erupting across the country, condemning the tax increase as "discriminatory robbery".

The opposition parties seized upon this public discontent, framing the budget as a symbol of the government's misplaced priorities and its failure to address the real concerns of ordinary citizens. They accused the government of fiscal mismanagement, claiming that the budget relied on record taxation revenues rather than sound financial management to achieve a temporary balance. The PSD launched a scathing attack on the government's economic policies, highlighting the increase in the tax burden on families already struggling with the rising cost of living.

The budget debate became a platform for the various political parties to articulate their visions for Portugal's future, revealing the stark ideological divides within the political spectrum. BE and the PCP called for greater investment in social programmes and measures to address inequality. Right-wing parties, including the PSD and the IL, advocated for lower taxes and a more business-friendly environment. The budget, ultimately approved by parliament solely with the votes of the ruling PS, exposed the fragility of the government's position and the growing challenges it faced in maintaining its authority.

The sale of the power solutions company Efacec to the German investment fund Mutares for €15 million, following a state investment of €395 million, became a lightning rod for criticism, further eroding public trust in the government. The opposition parties, united in their condemnation of the deal, accused the government of "burying €400 million" of taxpayers' money and demanded a parliamentary inquiry into an alleged lack of transparency surrounding the sale. The President expressed his disappointment with the "less than ideal" outcome, advising the government to clarify the terms of the sale, which fell "short of what was desired and believed possible".

Economy Minister António Costa Silva's defence of the privatisation, arguing that it was crucial for the country's sustainability and that the state would recoup a portion of its investment through dividends, failed to quell the mounting criticism. The opposition pointed to the lack of any immediate proceeds from the sale and the fact that any returns would be contingent on the company's future profitability. They demanded a parliamentary inquiry to scrutinise the deal and hold the government accountable for its perceived mishandling of the situation. The Efacec privatisation became a symbol of the government's perceived incompetence and its lack of transparency, further fuelling public discontent and adding to the growing sense of political instability.

The sudden resignation of Prime Minister Costa on 8 November sent shockwaves through Portuguese society, marking a dramatic culmination of a series of political scandals and the emergence of a major corruption investigation known as Operation Influencer. The investigation focused on allegations of corruption in the awarding of government contracts, including lithium mines, a hydrogen power plant and a data centre. Costa, while denying any wrongdoing, cited the "incompatibility between the dignity of his office and any suspicion of wrongdoing" as his reason for stepping down. This unexpected development triggered a political crisis, casting a long shadow over the future of the government and raising questions about the integrity of the political system.

Operation Influencer implicated several high-profile figures, including Costa's Chief of Staff Vítor Escária and Diogo Lacerda Machado, a lawyer allegedly close to Costa.

The investigation revealed allegations of bribery and illicit influence peddling, suggesting a network of corruption operating at the highest levels of government. The sources detail search warrants executed at the prime minister's official residence, the PS headquarters and locations linked to the lithium and hydrogen projects, uncovering evidence of "high-value meals and suspicious meetings".

The revelation of court-authorised taps on Costa's phone, recording conversations between the outgoing prime minister and key figures involved in the Operation Influencer investigation, further intensified the scandal. These phone taps revealed discussions about environmental licensing for the lithium mines and conversations with Infrastructure Minister Galamba, who was already a defendant in the case. The taps also provided information that led to a raid on Escária's office, where investigators seized €75,800 in cash.

The Operation Influencer investigation had a profound impact on public perception of the government, eroding trust in political institutions and fuelling a sense of disillusionment. The opposition parties, sensing an opportunity to capitalise on the crisis, called for President Rebelo de Sousa to dissolve parliament and call early elections, arguing that the government had lost its legitimacy. Costa's resignation and the unfolding corruption scandal cast a dark cloud over Portuguese politics, creating an atmosphere of uncertainty and raising questions about the country's future direction.

The resignation of Prime Minister Costa thrust President Rebelo de Sousa into the centre of the political storm, forcing him to make critical decisions regarding the future of the government. Faced with the unprecedented situation of a prime minister potentially implicated in a major corruption investigation, the President had to weigh the need for stability against the demands for accountability and transparency. His decision would shape the political landscape for the foreseeable future, impacting the upcoming general election and potentially altering the balance of power.

Mindful of the need to consult with all political actors, the President engaged in a series of meetings with the leaders of the parties represented in parliament. He also sought the advice of the Council of State, a body composed of prominent figures from various sectors of society, to gain a comprehensive understanding of the situation and the potential implications of his choices.

Rebelo de Sousa faced a complex dilemma: whether to allow the PS to nominate a new prime minister, potentially averting early elections, or to dissolve parliament and call for a fresh mandate from the people. This decision was further complicated by Costa's proposal to appoint Mário Centeno, Governor of the Bank of Portugal, as his successor. This suggestion was met with resistance from opposition parties, who argued that Centeno, while respected, had never held elected office so lacked the democratic legitimacy to lead the government.

Ultimately, the President decided to call early elections on 10 March 2024, rejecting Costa's recommendation to appoint Centeno and siding with the opposition parties that demanded a fresh start. He reasoned that the current government, tainted by the Operation Influencer scandal, had lost the public's trust and that new elections were necessary to restore confidence in the political system. This decision marked a pivotal moment in Portuguese politics, ushering in a period of uncertainty and setting the stage for a potentially transformative general election.

The resignation of Prime Minister Costa triggered a leadership contest within the PS, pitting two prominent figures against each other: José Luís Carneiro, representing the party's moderate wing, and Pedro Nuno Santos, seen as a champion of the left. This internal battle for the party's soul played out against the backdrop of the Operation Influencer scandal and the upcoming general election, adding another layer of complexity to the political landscape.

Carneiro, the incumbent Interior Minister, campaigned on a platform of stability and continuity, promising to uphold Costa's legacy while pursuing a more centrist approach. He emphasised the importance of dialogue with the opposition parties and pledged to avoid any pre-election coalitions with the far-right Chega. Santos, a former Infrastructure Minister who had resigned earlier in the year over a controversial payout to a TAP executive, presented himself as the candidate for change, advocating for a more progressive agenda and greater social justice. He sought to appeal to the PS's left-wing base, emphasising his commitment to tackling inequality and strengthening the welfare state.

The PS leadership contest became a microcosm of the broader political debate in Portugal, reflecting the tensions between continuity and change, moderation and radicalism. The outcome of this internal battle could have significant implications for the PS's electoral strategy and its ability to regain public trust in the wake of the Operation Influencer scandal.

The decision by President Rebelo de Sousa to call early elections set the stage for a pivotal political showdown as the parties prepared to vie for the electorate's support. The 10 March election promised to be a closely contested race, with the outcome holding significant consequences for the country's future direction.

The PSD, led by Luís Montenegro, sought to capitalise

on the government's woes, presenting itself as the party of change and stability. Montenegro pledged to restore public trust in institutions, tackle the healthcare crisis and implement economic policies that would benefit all Portuguese citizens. He ruled out any pre-election alliances with Chega, seeking to distance his party from the far-right and to appeal to moderate voters.

The PS, reeling from the Operation Influencer scandal and Costa's resignation, faced an uphill battle to retain its hold on power. The party's new leader, either Carneiro or Santos, would have to navigate the fallout from the scandal, rebuild public trust and articulate a compelling vision for the future. The outcome of the leadership contest would likely influence the PS's electoral strategy, determining whether the party would seek to continue Costa's legacy or chart a new course.

The general election, taking place against a backdrop of political uncertainty and economic challenges, promised to be a defining moment for a country at a crossroads and grappling with fundamental questions about its political future and the direction it wants to take.

Leadership challenges

December 2023 marked a period of significant political upheaval, characterised by a change in leadership for the ruling PS, the formation of a new centre-right coalition and lingering controversies surrounding the Lisbon airport project and allegations of presidential impropriety. These events set the stage for a potentially transformative election scheduled for 10 March 2024.

The month began with the political landscape still reeling from the fallout of Operation Influencer. The investigation implicated outgoing prime minister Costa, raising suspicions about his potential involvement in the affair. Although Costa maintained his innocence throughout, he ultimately chose to resign to avoid hindering the investigation. This decision triggered a series of political consequences, leaving the government in a caretaker role with limited authority and creating uncertainty about critical policy decisions, including the future of the long-debated Lisbon airport project.

Costa's resignation necessitated a leadership election for the PS. Three candidates emerged: Santos, Carneiro and Daniel Adrião. Santos, the former Infrastructure and Housing Minister, positioned himself as a representative of the party's left wing, advocating state intervention and a strong welfare state. He pledged to restore teacher seniority lost during the pandemic, a promise that later faced scrutiny for its financial feasibility. Carneiro, the Interior Minister, presented himself as a figure of moderation and stability. He enjoyed the backing of Costa's inner circle and emphasised his ability to win elections and maintain the PS's "strategic autonomy". Adrião, a lesser-known figure, championed greater internal party democracy and grassroots participation.

The leadership contest was ultimately won by Santos with a decisive 62% of the vote. His victory signalled a generational shift within the PS, as younger party members ascended to positions of influence. However, Santos' victory speech was criticised by some for lacking substance and focusing primarily on attacking the main opposition PSD.

The PSD under Montenegro sought to capitalise on the political instability created by Costa's resignation. Montenegro's strategy centred on forging pre-election alliances with other right-wing parties to unseat the PS and curb the growing influence of the far-right Chega party. This approach drew criticism from some quarters for potentially legitimising Chega and for its lack of a clearly defined policy platform.

Montenegro's efforts culminated in the establishment of the Democratic Alliance (AD—Aliança Democrática), a coalition with the PP. The AD, positioned as a "reformist and moderate" force, aimed to consolidate the centre-right vote and present a united front against the PS. The coalition agreement also extended to regional and municipal elections.

The AD's formation elicited mixed reactions. Chega leader Ventura dismissed it as a "gift for the PS", while IL expressed confidence in its ability to succeed independently. The PCP, recalling the austerity measures implemented during the troika era, reminded voters of the PSD-PP alliance's past performance and urged those disillusioned with the PS to vote PCP instead.

Two major controversies continued to cast a shadow over Portuguese politics throughout December: the ongoing debate surrounding the location of Lisbon's new airport and allegations of presidential favouritism in a medical case.

After much anticipation, the Independent Technical Commission announced its recommendation for the new airport, selecting Alcochete as the preferred site. However, this decision sparked immediate political disagreement and revealed logistical challenges. The PSD formed a working group to re-evaluate the proposal, effectively delaying a final decision. Santos criticised the delay and called for swift action. The Alcochete option also faced opposition from tourism organisations and airport operator ANA, which favoured the Montijo project due to its perceived feasibility and cost-effectiveness.

The second controversy centred on allegations that President Marcelo Rebelo de Sousa had used his influence to secure costly medical treatment for twin girls with spinal muscular atrophy. The President acknowledged that his son had contacted him requesting intervention but denied any direct involvement or favouritism. The controversy intensified when documents emerged suggesting the Health Ministry's involvement. This led to calls for a parliamentary hearing and cast a pall over the presidency.

Throughout December, opinion polls provided snapshots of the evolving political landscape. Despite undergoing a leadership transition, the PS maintained its lead over the PSD. Chega continued to gain support, solidifying its position as the third most popular party. However, public confidence in both Santos and Montenegro remained low, highlighting the challenges confronting both leaders as they geared up for the March elections.

The pre-election campaign was characterised by sharp exchanges between the main parties. Santos emphasised the PS's commitment to a strong welfare state and criticised the PSD's alleged embrace of radicalism and its potential reliance on Chega's support. Montenegro, in turn, accused Santos of mismanagement during his tenure as Infrastructure Minister, particularly regarding the national airline TAP. He also attempted to distance the PSD from Chega, insisting that the far-right party would play no role in a PSD-led government.

Chega continued its assertive campaign, highlighting issues such as immigration and criticising both the PS and PSD for their perceived "blandness". Ventura stated that his party would only support a minority PSD government if it implemented Chega's desired policies. He also suggested that the PSD should negotiate with the PS if Montenegro refused to deal with Chega.

The events of December 2023 laid the groundwork for a potentially decisive election in March 2024. The PS under Santos sought to maintain its hold on power, emphasising its commitment to social welfare and economic stability.

The PSD, in coalition with the PP, aimed to unseat the PS and present itself as a viable alternative, while navigating the complexities of its relationship with Chega. The rise of Chega, the lingering controversies surrounding the Lisbon airport project and presidential conduct and the persistent economic challenges facing Portugal ensured the political landscape remained volatile and unpredictable.

Portugal at a crossroads

The year 2023 in Portugal was not merely a sequence of events; it was a crucible, a period of intense pressure that exposed the fault lines within the nation's political system, its economic structures and its social fabric.

What began as a seemingly stable political landscape, marked by a comfortable PS majority, ended in a dramatic political implosion, with a government brought to its knees by a relentless cascade of scandals, public discontent and, ultimately, its own internal contradictions. The events of this year serve not just as a chronicle of a nation in turmoil but as a cautionary tale about the fragility of power, the corrosive nature of unchecked authority and the enduring importance of transparency, accountability and a responsive government. The year's narrative arc is defined by a steady erosion of public trust, punctuated by a series of crises that exposed deep-seated systemic weaknesses. The TAP Air Portugal scandal, the Galambagate affair, the controversial More Housing Programme and the Operation Influencer corruption investigation were not isolated incidents; they were interconnected threads in a tapestry of governmental dysfunction. The TAP affair, with its revelations of excessive compensation, financial irregularities and political interference, set the stage for the year's subsequent dramas. This was more than just a financial scandal; it was a potent symbol of a government seemingly disconnected from the concerns of ordinary citizens, prioritising political expediency over sound governance. The dismissals of TAP's chief executive and chairman, Christine Ourmières-Widener and Manuel Beja, while meant to quell public anger, were largely viewed as scapegoating attempts, further undermining faith in political accountability.

The ensuing parliamentary inquiry into TAP became a battleground of competing narratives. While the government sought to downplay its involvement, opposition parties and media revelations painted a picture of an airline operating under political pressure and a government attempting to obstruct scrutiny. The inquiry's findings, while not directly implicating government ministers in criminal wrongdoing, nevertheless underscored the systemic weaknesses in the governance of state-owned enterprises and raised serious questions about the intersection of politics and business. The controversy over the secret meetings between PS MPs and TAP executives before their parliamentary testimony further exacerbated the sense of a system manipulated for political advantage, contributing to a growing cynicism among the electorate.

The Galambagate affair that followed, represented a

new level of political drama. The allegations of ministerial misconduct, the involvement of the SIS, and the conflicting testimonies from government officials created a sense of a government operating in a climate of dishonesty and secrecy. Prime Minister Costa's unwavering support for Infrastructure Minister Galamba, despite mounting evidence of wrongdoing, became a flashpoint in the political arena. This decision not only strained the relationship between the Prime Minister and President Rebelo de Sousa, but also reinforced the perception of a government unwilling to hold its own members accountable.

The More Housing Programme, intended to address the nation's growing housing crisis, backfired spectacularly, becoming another symbol of the government's disconnect from reality. While the intention may have been to alleviate the suffering of those priced out of the housing market, the programme's controversial measures, particularly the "compulsory lease" scheme, sparked widespread criticism from all sides. The opposition parties and even the President expressed concerns over the practicality and fairness of the programme, arguing it would only serve to exacerbate the housing crisis by infringing on fundamental property rights. This situation revealed a government seemingly out of touch with public opinion and unable to navigate complex policy issues with care and nuance.

The government's failures were not merely restricted to specific scandals or policy missteps; they also manifested in its response to broader societal crises. The healthcare system, already under strain, spiralled into a full-blown crisis, marked by a chronic shortage of doctors, widespread A&E closures and increasing public anxiety. While the government insisted that it had allocated adequate funding to the national health service (SNS), its response was widely criticised as reactive and insufficient. The proposal to recruit doctors from Cuba, while intended to address the immediate shortages, raised ethical concerns and further fueled public discontent. The Doctors in Protest movement highlighted the deep-seated frustrations within the health profession, revealing a system stretched to its limits and unable to cope with the demands of a growing and ageing population.

The economic anxieties of ordinary Portuguese citizens also reached a fever pitch in 2023. The cost-of-living crisis, exacerbated by soaring inflation and rising housing costs, placed immense strain on households across the country. The government's attempts to mitigate the impact of these crises, such as the introduction of a temporary zero VAT rate on essential food items, were largely perceived as inadequate and short-term solutions that failed to address the underlying structural problems. The concerns about the management of the economy and the perceived lack of transparency also further eroded trust in the government's credibility.

The resignation of Prime Minister Costa in November marked the dramatic culmination of this year of political turmoil. The Operation Influencer investigation, with its allegations of corruption, bribery and influence peddling at the highest levels of government, finally brought the house of cards down. While Costa denied any wrongdoing, the fact that the investigation implicated him and his inner circle proved to be the final straw. His resignation, while triggered by a specific corruption scandal, was also the product of months of accumulated mistrust, public anger and a sense that the government had lost its moral authority. The situation was such that a resignation, which in other circumstances may have appeased public anger, was seen by many as too little, too late.

The manner of Costa's departure, seemingly forced

upon him by the weight of the scandal rather than a genuine acceptance of responsibility, further contributed to the sense of a political system failing its citizens. The decision by President Rebelo de Sousa to call early elections, rather than allow the PS to nominate a successor, was a clear indication that the government had lost the public's mandate. This rejection of Costa's proposed successor further underscored the perception of a political class deeply entangled in self-serving agendas and out of touch with the needs of the people.

The events of 2023 also had a profound impact on the broader political landscape. The rise of the populist right-wing Chega party, led by André Ventura, was a clear indication of the growing public discontent with the political establishment. Chega's anti-establishment rhetoric, its focus on issues such as immigration and its attacks on perceived corruption resonated with a segment of the population that felt disenfranchised and forgotten. While PSD leader Montenegro consistently ruled out any alliance with Chega, the party's growing influence underscored the shifting dynamics within the right-wing bloc and raised questions about the future of Portuguese politics. The emergence of smaller parties, such as PAN and Livre, also marked a fragmentation of the established political system, reflecting a growing desire among voters for alternative voices.

The relationship between the ruling PS and the left-wing BE also underwent a significant transformation. The election of Mariana Mortágua as the BE's new leader signaled a more critical and confrontational stance towards the government, reflecting a broader disillusionment among left-wing voters with the PS's policies. The traditional alliance between the PS and BE, often characterised by compromise and cooperation, was replaced by a more adversarial approach, further fragmenting the political landscape and making a clear path forward for a new government difficult to envision.

President Rebelo de Sousa's role in the year's unfolding events also deserves scrutiny. While a largely ceremonial position, he used the presidency to exert pressure on the government, acting as a check on executive power and reflecting a more assertive approach to the constitutional role of the President. His criticisms of the government, his interventions in policy debates and his eventual decision to call early elections all underscored his willingness to challenge the status quo and hold the government accountable, despite constraints on his executive power. While many lauded his attempts to act as a bulwark against government excess, others criticised him for overstepping the mark and acting more like an opposition leader than a neutral head of state.

As the year came to a close, Portugal found itself at a critical juncture. The events of 2023 exposed deep-seated weaknesses in its democratic institutions, its economic structures, and its political culture. The legacy of this year will be a lingering sense of mistrust in government and a desire for greater transparency, accountability, and ethical standards in public life. The March 2024 elections were poised to be a defining moment for the nation, with voters facing the challenge of choosing a new direction for their country. The question that remained at the end of 2023 was whether the lessons of this tumultuous year would be heeded, and if the new leadership would be able to rebuild trust, restore stability, and address the underlying challenges that led to such profound political upheaval.

Ultimately, 2023 in Portugal was a year of unravelling. It was the year when the carefully constructed narratives of stability and progress crumbled under the weight of corruption scandals, economic hardship and government dysfunction. The story of 2023 is a story of contrasts and contradictions: of a government elected with a mandate for stability, only to be brought down by its own internal weaknesses; of a society struggling to reconcile its traditional values with the demands of the modern world; of a people yearning for change but uncertain about the future. This is a year that will undoubtedly have long-lasting consequences for Portugal and its place in the world. It's not simply a matter of moving past this challenging year, but understanding why such a fundamental breakdown of trust occurred and what steps are needed to ensure it is never repeated.

The events of 2023 revealed the complex and often contradictory nature of Portuguese society, with its tensions between tradition and modernity, social justice and economic progress, stability and change. The legacy of 2023 will continue to shape the nation's trajectory for years to come, a constant reminder of the importance of transparency, accountability and a political system that truly serves the needs of its citizens. This is no small challenge, and the path ahead will undoubtedly be marked by challenges and divisions.

Appendices

TAP Air Portugal

This scandal, which unfolded in early 2023, is a powerful illustration of the political turbulence and public discontent gripping Portugal then. This complex affair, centring on a controversial compensation package given to a former executive, quickly escalated into a full-blown crisis, exposing deep-seated issues of transparency, accountability and ethical conduct within the government and the national airline. The repercussions of the scandal reverberated throughout the year, contributing to a significant erosion of public trust in political institutions and setting the stage for further political upheaval.

At the heart of the controversy lay a €500,000 compensation payment made to Alexandra Reis, a former executive of TAP Air Portugal, upon her departure from the airline's board. This payment, deemed excessively generous and potentially illegal by many, became a focal point for public anger and political scrutiny. The situation was further complicated by the fact that Reis had subsequently held government positions, raising serious questions about potential conflicts of interest and the lack of proper oversight. The sheer scale of the compensation, especially in light of TAP's financial difficulties and its status as a state-owned entity, sparked outrage and demands for accountability.

The initial revelations about the compensation package triggered a swift political response. Pedro Nuno Santos, then the Minister of Infrastructure and Housing, who had overseen TAP, resigned from his post in the wake of the scandal. His departure marked the first in a series of ministerial resignations that would plague the government throughout the year, creating a sense of instability and highlighting the fragility of Prime Minister Costa's administration. The resignation of Santos, a prominent figure within the ruling PS, sent shockwaves through the political establishment and signalled the seriousness of the situation.

Following Santos' resignation, the Attorney General's Office launched a formal inquiry into the legality of the compensation payment. This investigation aimed to determine whether any laws had been broken and to identify those responsible for authorising the payment. The fact the country's top legal authority had to step in indicated the gravity of the situation and further intensified scrutiny of the government's actions. The opposition parties, sensing an opportunity to gain political advantage, launched scathing attacks on the government, calling for further resignations, including that of Finance Minister Medina, and demanding a full and transparent investigation into the matter. The opposition parties sought to portray the government as being out of touch with public concerns and tolerating or encouraging corrupt practices.

Prime Minister Costa, facing mounting pressure from all sides, acknowledged that Reis had likely broken the law by accepting a position on the Portuguese Air Navigation Company (NAV) board without returning part of the compensation she had received from TAP. This admission, while an attempt to address public concerns, did little to quell the rising tide of criticism. Instead, it fuelled accusations of government mismanagement, a lack of transparency and an apparent culture of impunity within the ruling PS party.

As the scandal continued to unfold, revelations about Reis's subsequent appointments further undermined the government's credibility. The fact that someone who had received such a large sum of money from a state-owned company could then take up another position in the public sector without any apparent repercussions raised serious questions about the government's oversight and vetting procedures. These issues exposed a lack of institutional safeguards, allowing individuals to benefit from their positions within the state and eroding public trust in the integrity of the political system.

The TAP affair also served as a catalyst for broader concerns about the management of state-owned enterprises. The scandal highlighted how government policies and decisions can affect public funds, and how this lack of oversight can lead to significant losses. It also underscored how decisions made by politically appointed individuals are difficult to challenge and can result in substantial sums of public money being spent with minimal accountability. The lack of transparency in the compensation agreement with Reis was symptomatic of a larger problem: a failure to ensure that public institutions operate fairly and transparently. The scandal revealed a system that was vulnerable to political interference and lacked the checks and balances necessary to safeguard public resources.

The repercussions of the TAP scandal extended beyond the immediate political sphere, impacting the leadership and prospects of the airline. The scandal directly led to the dismissal of TAP chief executive officer Christine Ourmières-Widener and chairman Manuel Beja. While presented as a necessary response to the crisis, these dismissals were also criticised by some as a scapegoating exercise, with the opposition accusing the government of shielding those higher up the chain of command. Ourmières-Widener vehemently contested her dismissal, threatening legal action and demanding full payment of her salary and potential bonuses. This legal battle added another layer of complexity to the situation and underscored the potential financial implications of the scandal for the airline.

The Court of Auditors also became involved, contemplating imposing fines on both Ourmières-Widener and Beja for potential financial infractions, which only added to the uncertainty surrounding the airline's future. The sheer amount of public scrutiny and the uncertainty surrounding its management led to a significant decline in public confidence in the national carrier and its ability to operate successfully. The saga exposed the fragility of a major public asset and the impact of a political scandal on a key component of the Portuguese economy.

The political fallout from the TAP affair was far-reaching and damaging for the government. The scandal exposed deep divisions within the ruling PS and led to the departure of several prominent figures. The successive resignations of ministers and secretaries of state, stemming from ethical lapses and potential criminal wrongdoing, painted a damning picture of the government. The scandal eroded public trust and intensified calls for accountability. The perception of widespread corruption and a culture of impunity within the government contributed to a growing disillusionment among the Portuguese public.

The opposition parties, sensing an opportunity to capitalise on the government's vulnerabilities, were quick to condemn the government's actions and call for further resignations and investigations. They framed the scandal as evidence of the government's incompetence and its failure to uphold the highest standards of public service. The scandal became a rallying cry for opposition parties across the political spectrum, fuelling anti-government sentiment and contributing to a more polarised political landscape. The ongoing criticism and demands for accountability added to the pressure on Prime Minister Costa and his administration.

The TAP saga also had an impact on the role of President Rebelo de Sousa, who emerged as a vocal critic of the government's handling of the crisis. In his New Year's message, the President urged Prime Minister Costa to address the political instability and bolster the country's economic resilience. He also gave Costa one year to "get his house in order", warning that he would not rule out calling for early elections should a credible alternative emerge. The President's intervention injected a sense of urgency into the political landscape and exerted further pressure on Costa to restore public confidence and highlighted the importance of his role as a check on government power and the fragility of the political system.

Despite the government's attempts to regain control of the narrative, the TAP scandal continued to dominate the political discourse throughout the year. Prime Minister Costa attempted to stabilise his government by reshuffling his cabinet and introducing a new vetting process for ministerial appointments. However, these efforts were met with scepticism from opposition parties and the public who viewed them as inadequate and insufficient to address the underlying issues of accountability and transparency. It also emerged that six current ministers would have failed the proposed vetting process, further highlighting the government's vulnerability and the depth of its issues.

The TAP Air Portugal scandal stands as a watershed moment in Portuguese politics. The affair laid bare serious flaws within the government and a lack of public trust in state-owned institutions. The scandal began with a controversial payment and became a symbol of government mismanagement and a lack of accountability. The scale of the scandal, the number of resignations and the political fall-out, including the President's involvement, showed the governing coalition's fragility. The TAP saga became a focal point for opposition parties and contributed to the erosion of public trust in the country's political leadership and had implications for the future direction of Portuguese politics.

More Housing Programme

The housing crisis that gripped Portugal in early 2023 and the government's subsequent attempts to address it through its More Housing Programme became a central point of political contention and public debate. This crisis, characterised by skyrocketing property prices, a dwindling supply of rental properties and widespread public frustration, exposed deep-seated socio-economic challenges within the country and tested the government's capacity to provide effective solutions. The government's response to the crisis, whilst seemingly well-intentioned, ignited fierce debate, highlighting the complex interplay between economic policy, social welfare and political considerations.

The housing crisis had been simmering for some

time, with property prices in Portugal increasing dramatically in recent years, driven by a combination of factors, including foreign investment, short-term tourist rentals and a lack of affordable housing options for ordinary citizens. This situation led to a growing sense of injustice, with many Portuguese people finding it increasingly difficult to secure decent housing. The issue became particularly acute in major urban centres, such as Lisbon and Porto, where rental prices soared to levels that were often unaffordable for the average worker. This created a situation of social inequality, pushing many families to the margins and fuelling public anger. The severity of the situation meant that the government had little choice but to act.

In February, the government unveiled its More Housing Programme, a comprehensive package of measures designed to alleviate the crisis. This programme targeted various aspects of the housing market, including rent controls, restrictions on short-term rentals, financial assistance for tenants and homeowners and controversial measures to compel owners of vacant properties to rent them out. While the government presented the programme as a bold and necessary step towards solving the housing crisis, it quickly became a lightning rod for criticism and debate. The programme's ambition was to address several challenges simultaneously, but the complexity of the proposed solutions made it a difficult political proposition.

One of the most contentious elements of the More Housing Programme was the compulsory lease scheme allowing the state to take administrative possession of vacant properties under certain circumstances. This proposal sparked a fierce debate, with critics, including former PS ministers, questioning its legality and effectiveness. Many saw the scheme as an infringement on property rights and a potentially authoritarian overreach of government power, while others argued the measures were necessary to ensure that properties were not left vacant at a time of acute housing shortage. This aspect of the plan became a focal point for opposition parties, which accused Prime Minister Costa of adopting a "communist" approach and undermining the principles of a free market economy.

Another controversial aspect of the programme was the proposed restrictions on short-term rentals, designed to free up properties for long-term residents. This measure, aimed at curbing the boom in tourist accommodation, sparked protests from those involved in the tourism sector who argued that such restrictions would significantly damage their livelihoods and negatively impact the country's tourism industry. This highlighted the tension between the need to address the housing crisis and the need to protect the interests of a vital economic sector. The government struggled to find a balance between competing interests and its solution alienated both sides of the argument.

Beyond these specific measures, the More Housing Programme as a whole faced criticism for failing to address the underlying structural factors driving the crisis. Opposition parties argued that the programme was too superficial, focusing on symptoms rather than addressing the root causes of the housing crisis and that it did little to address wage stagnation, which was exacerbating the problem of housing affordability.

Opposition parties, notably the PSD and BE, swiftly condemned the programme, arguing that it failed to adequately address the fundamental factors driving the housing crisis. PSD leader Luís Montenegro lambasted the plan as "perverse and wrong," accusing Prime Minister Costa of adopting a communist approach by proposing such measures. BE MP Mariana Mortágua echoed these criticisms, asserting that the plan would have negligible impact and would not deter continued protests, emphasising that people urgently need affordable housing solutions.

The government's decision to open the More Housing Programme to public consultation until 10 March suggested a willingness to consider revisions. However, this did little to quell public dissatisfaction, with people doubting the government's commitment to finding a real solution to the crisis. There was also a general feeling that the programme did not have the public's best interest at heart and was more concerned with political posturing.

The housing crisis and the government's attempts to address it also had an impact on the relationship between the government and the President, Rebelo de Sousa. The President, who had previously emerged as a vocal critic of the government's handling of the TAP scandal, continued to act as a check on executive power. He denounced the Programme and threatened to veto the forced lease scheme. His public criticism of the Programme was a powerful rebuke to the government and further undermined its credibility. This intervention further highlighted the divisions between the government and the President and added complexity to an already difficult situation.

As the year went on, the housing crisis remained a pressing concern for many Portuguese citizens, with the cost-of-living crisis only making the matter more urgent. A Catholic University poll revealed the extent of the crisis, indicating that one in four Portuguese individuals had struggled to afford necessities like food, medication and household expenses in the past year. The government's attempts to address the crisis were often met with scepticism, with many feeling that it was not doing enough to alleviate the burden on ordinary families.

The More Housing Programme became a lightning

rod for public frustration, highlighting the government's perceived inability to solve a pressing social issue effectively. Its unveiling coincided with reports of a growing number of people without access to a family doctor and of A&E departments struggling to cope. These compounding crises contributed to a sense of unease and raised questions about the government's capacity to address the needs of ordinary citizens.

The government did try to ease the burden on citizens by introducing mechanisms designed to stabilise mortgage payments and prevent sudden increases due to rising interest rates. The government also introduced a range of other measures, including tax exemptions for young workers and free public transport for those under 23. However, these measures were often seen as insufficient and did little to quell the broader discontent over the housing market and the government's response to it.

By September 2023, the housing crisis had reached a critical point, with the government and the President in open conflict over its proposed solutions. President Rebelo de Sousa's decision to veto the Programme further exacerbated the situation, creating a sense of political instability and uncertainty. While the government was able to pass the legislation at the second time of asking, this did little to ease public concern over the matter. This also led to an increase in political tensions, as the President publicly criticised the government for its handling of the matter.

In October, the European Commission rejected Prime Minister Costa's request for additional support and tools to address the housing crisis, advising Lisbon to address the problem internally. This rejection placed the onus firmly on the Portuguese government to find practical solutions, amplifying the pressure on Costa and his administration.

This rejection also underscored the feeling that the government failed to address a problem with far-reaching consequences for Portuguese society.

By November, the situation had become so critical that it contributed to the resignation of Prime Minister Costa. The resignation of the Prime Minister signalled the culmination of a series of scandals and crises that had beset the government throughout the year. While Costa was implicated in Operation Influencer, the housing crisis was one of several key factors that led to public discontent and political instability. The resignation of Costa also served as a catalyst for further political upheaval, setting the stage for early elections in March 2024.

The housing crisis in Portugal in 2023 was a complex issue that exposed deep-seated socio-economic problems and tested the government's ability to provide effective solutions. The More Housing Programme, while intended to address the crisis, became a focal point of political controversy, further highlighting the divisions between the government, opposition parties and the President. The crisis highlighted the challenges of balancing competing interests, managing public expectations and responding to complex socio-economic issues in a politically charged environment. It also underscored the fragility of the political system and the erosion of public trust in the country's leadership.

Galambagate

The Galambagate scandal, which unfolded in May, was a complex web of accusations, political manoeuvring and institutional clashes that significantly shook the foundations of the government. At its heart lay a dispute involving the then Infrastructure Minister, João Galamba, and his former assistant, Frederico Pinheiro, but its ramifications extended far beyond this initial conflict, raising serious questions about government transparency, accountability and the relationship between the executive branch and other state institutions.

The saga began with Pinheiro's dismissal, ostensibly for "behaviour incompatible with his duties and responsibilities". However, Pinheiro countered by alleging that

Galamba had instructed him to lie to the parliamentary inquiry investigating the national airline, TAP. This was a particularly sensitive issue given the ongoing scrutiny of TAP's management and the numerous controversies that had already engulfed the airline. Adding another layer of complexity, Pinheiro was accused of removing computers containing classified information from the ministry premises. This act triggered the involvement of the Security Intelligence Service (SIS), Portugal's intelligence agency, which was tasked with recovering the missing equipment. This unusual step, using the SIS for what many considered a police matter, immediately raised eyebrows and fuelled further speculation about the government's motives.

The use of the SIS became a major point of contention. Prime Minister Costa defended the SIS's involvement, arguing that it was necessary to protect classified information. However, this explanation failed to satisfy critics, who questioned why the police hadn't been involved from the outset and what was so sensitive that it required the intervention of the intelligence services. Opposition parties and the public became increasingly concerned about the potential for misuse of power and the blurring of lines between political expediency and institutional integrity. This concern was compounded by the fact that the SIS is not generally involved in such cases.

The situation escalated further when President Rebelo de Sousa reportedly told Costa that Galamba could no longer remain in the government. The President, a figurehead respected across the political spectrum, expressed serious concerns about the damage the scandal was causing to the credibility of the state. Despite the President's intervention and an offer of resignation from Galamba, Prime Minister Costa stood firmly by his minister. This defiant stance created an open rift between the President and the

Prime Minister, a highly unusual occurrence in Portuguese politics, highlighting the severity of the crisis and the deep divisions it had exposed. The President's decision not to dissolve parliament or dismiss the government at this point was "for the sake of stability", but he issued a stern warning to the government, criticising its "unreliability and lack of respectability", suggesting that he would be more closely involved with the government's function moving forward. This unprecedented step by the President underscored the gravity of the situation and placed the Costa government under increased scrutiny.

As the scandal unfolded, more details emerged, further complicating the picture. It was revealed that Galamba had allegedly coached former TAP chief executive Christine Ourmières-Widener ahead of her appearance at a parliamentary hearing. This raised questions about the fairness and integrity of the inquiry into TAP, given that Galamba was involved in the issues being investigated. Further allegations of misconduct and attempts to cover up evidence surfaced during subsequent hearings, particularly from Pinheiro and Galamba's chief of staff, Eugénia Correia. These developments kept the scandal in the public eye and fuelled ongoing criticism of the government's transparency and accountability.

The TAP inquiry itself became another focal point of political tension. Opposition parties accused the government of obstructing its work and shielding key figures from scrutiny. The PS, in turn, rejected opposition requests for Prime Minister Costa and other senior figures to testify, arguing that their testimonies were outside the scope of the investigation. This back-and-forth highlighted the partisan nature of the crisis and the challenges of obtaining a complete and impartial account of the events surrounding TAP.

The Galambagate scandal was not an isolated incident but rather part of a series of controversies and scandals that plagued the government in 2023. These included the Alexandra Reis compensation scandal involving TAP, the More Housing Programme controversies and various allegations of corruption and ethical violations. The cumulative effect of these scandals was to erode public trust in the political system and fuel a sense of disillusionment among citizens. The Galambagate scandal, however, stood out because of the direct clash between the Prime Minister and the President, and its implications for the checks and balances in Portuguese democracy.

The scandal exposed a pattern of what some critics describe as the government's tendency towards opacity and a lack of transparency. The use of the SIS in the Pinheiro case, the allegations of coaching witnesses and the government's perceived obstruction of the TAP inquiry all contributed to this narrative. This was not just a matter of political point-scoring, it raised genuine concerns about how the government conducts its affairs, who it answers to and whether the country's institutions were being undermined.

The political fallout from Galambagate was significant. The scandal took a toll on the popularity of the ruling PS, with opinion polls showing a decline in their support. The opposition parties, particularly the PSD and BE, seized upon the opportunity to attack the government and call for Galamba's resignation. The scandal also intensified the debate about the need for greater accountability and transparency in government and the importance of independent institutions that could hold those in power to account.

In the broader context of Portuguese politics, the Galambagate scandal highlighted the growing tensions between the ruling PS and the opposition parties and the president's increasing assertiveness. The scandal also provided further ammunition to the rising populist right-wing Chega party, which capitalised on public discontent and anxieties surrounding the government's handling of various crises.

Galambagate had far-reaching implications. It was not just about an infrastructure minister and his former assistant; it was about the integrity of the Portuguese government and the relationship between its various institutions. The scandal demonstrated how a seemingly isolated incident can quickly escalate into a major political crisis, highlighting the importance of transparency, accountability and the rule of law. It also revealed the deep divisions within Portuguese society and the growing public disillusionment with the political establishment. It revealed a culture of mistrust between the government and the public. It raised questions about the ability of the government to govern effectively and in the best interests of its citizens.

In conclusion, Galambagate was a stark reminder of the fragility of political power and the importance of maintaining public trust. The scandal's lasting impact lies in the political manoeuvring and institutional clashes it exposed and in its contribution to a growing sense of unease and uncertainty within Portuguese society. The events of May 2023 served as a catalyst for a deeper reflection on the state of Portuguese democracy and the need for a more accountable and transparent government. The scandal also paved the way for further political turmoil, culminating in Prime Minister Costa's resignation in November. The consequences of this scandal continue to be felt within the Portuguese political sphere.

Costa resigns

The resignation of António Costa as prime minister in November marked a dramatic turning point in Portuguese politics, triggering a period of uncertainty and setting the stage for a snap general election. Costa's departure was not the result of a policy disagreement or electoral defeat; instead, it was the culmination of a series of scandals and controversies that had plagued his government throughout the year, ultimately culminating in a major corruption investigation known as Operation Influencer. This event sent shockwaves through the country, raising profound questions about government integrity, transparency and the future direction of Portuguese politics.

The seeds of Costa's downfall were sown months before his resignation, as his government faced criticism over its handling of various issues. The TAP Air Portugal scandal, involving a controversial compensation payment to a former executive, had already triggered ministerial resignations and fuelled public anger. The government's attempts to address the housing crisis with the More Housing Programme were also met with widespread criticism and public scepticism. These controversies, coupled with a series of other ethical lapses and allegations of corruption, eroded public trust in the government and diminished Costa's authority. The Galambagate scandal, as we have already discussed, was a significant contributor to this decline in public trust, highlighting a perceived lack of transparency and accountability within the government and a major clash between the Prime Minister and the President.

However, Operation Influencer ultimately triggered Costa's resignation. This investigation focused on allegations of corruption in awarding government contracts, including those related to lithium mining, a hydrogen power plant, and a data centre. The investigation implicated several high-profile figures, including Costa's Chief of Staff, Vítor Escária, and a lawyer with close ties to the Prime Minister, Diogo Lacerda Machado. The specific accusations included bribery and illicit influence peddling, suggesting a network of corruption that reached the highest levels of government.

The details of the investigation, which were made public through various media reports, painted a damning picture of the government's conduct. Search warrants were executed at the Prime Minister's official residence, the PS headquarters and locations linked to the lithium and hydrogen projects, revealing evidence of "high-value meals and suspicious meetings". These searches were part of a coordinated effort to gather evidence of wrongdoing, and they immediately cast a shadow over Costa and his administration.

Adding further weight to the allegations, it was revealed that court-authorised taps had been placed on Costa's phone. These phone conversations between Costa and key figures in the Operation Influencer investigation revealed discussions about environmental licensing for the lithium mines and conversations with Infrastructure Minister Galamba, who was already implicated in other scandals. These tapped conversations provided crucial information to the investigators and significantly heightened public concern about the government's integrity. The taps also led to a raid on Escária's office, where investigators seized significant cash (€75,800). These discoveries created a sense of crisis and underscored the seriousness of the allegations against the government.

Faced with these damning revelations and amid mounting public and political pressure, Costa chose to resign from his position on 8 November 2023. Although he denied any personal wrongdoing, he stated that the "incompatibility between the dignity of his office and any suspicion of wrongdoing" made it impossible for him to continue as prime minister. This decision, while perhaps aimed at preserving his own reputation, had significant consequences for Portuguese politics and triggered a major political crisis.

Costa's resignation plunged the country into a period of uncertainty. The government was reduced to a caretaker role with limited authority. The decision to hold an early election on 10 March 2024 resulted from the political crisis sparked by the Operation Influencer investigation and the prime minister's departure. This meant that critical policy decisions, including the long-debated Lisbon airport project, were put on hold. The nation was left in political limbo, with no clear direction and the key policy decisions on hold.

The fallout from Costa's resignation extended far beyond the immediate political crisis. His departure led to a leadership contest within the PS. Two prominent figures emerged as candidates: José Luís Carneiro, representing the party's moderate wing, and Pedro Nuno Santos, a champion of the left. This internal struggle reflected a deeper ideological divide within the party, and the outcome of the leadership contest was expected to significantly influence the PS's electoral strategy and its ability to regain public trust following the scandals. In the end, Santos won the leadership contest.

The resignation of the Prime Minister had a profound impact on public perception of the government, eroding trust in political institutions and fuelling a sense of disillusionment. The opposition parties, particularly the PSD and the right-wing populist party Chega, seized the opportunity to attack the government and demand early elections. They argued that the government had lost its legitimacy and that a fresh mandate from the people was needed to restore confidence in the political system. The PSD subsequently formed a coalition with the PP to contest the upcoming general election.

The events surrounding Costa's resignation also highlighted the fragility of political power and the importance of maintaining public trust. The Operation Influencer scandal was not an isolated incident; it was the culmination of a series of ethical lapses, allegations of corruption and questionable government decisions. The cumulative effect of these events was to erode public faith in the political establishment and fuel a sense of unease and uncertainty within Portuguese society.

The resignation of the Prime Minister and the subsequent political crisis also brought into sharp focus the role of the President of the Republic, Rebelo de Sousa. While largely a ceremonial figurehead, the President is empowered to dissolve parliament and call early elections. In this case, President Rebelo de Sousa was forced to make a critical decision about the future of the government. The President opted to call the early elections. His decision was made after a series of meetings with the various political actors in the country and in consultation with the Council of State, and it was widely seen as the only way to restore public confidence in the country's political institutions.

The events leading up to and following Costa's resignation underscored the deep divisions within Portuguese society. The political landscape was characterised by the growing influence of the populist right-wing Chega party, the ongoing tensions between the PS and the opposition parties, and the increasing assertiveness of the President. These divisions were exacerbated by the various scandals and controversies that plagued the government and the economic challenges facing the country. The upcoming general election promised to be a closely contested race, with the outcome likely to have significant implications for the country's future direction.

António Costa's resignation was the culmination of a series of events that exposed the fragility of the Portuguese political system and the importance of maintaining public trust. The Operation Influencer investigation, with its allegations of corruption and illicit influence peddling, was the final straw that led to his departure. His resignation triggered a major political crisis, leading to an early general election and forcing a period of deep reflection on the state of Portuguese democracy and the need for a more accountable and transparent government.

Early elections

The lead-up to the early general election in Portugal, scheduled for 10 March 2024, was a period of intense political manoeuvring, shifting alliances, and public uncertainty, all stemming from Prime Minister Costa's dramatic resignation in November 2023. The months preceding the election were marked by a series of events, scandals, and political realignments that profoundly shaped the electoral landscape and left the country grappling with questions about its future direction.

The immediate catalyst for the early election was, of course, the Operation Influencer corruption scandal that led to Costa's resignation. As discussed previously, this investigation into allegations of bribery and influence peddling in the awarding of government contracts involving high-profile figures within the PS government sent shockwaves through the country. The scandal triggered Costa's departure and severely damaged the public's trust in the political establishment, creating a vacuum that opposition parties were eager to fill. The government was reduced to a caretaker role with limited authority, which intensified the instability and made an early election seem increasingly inevitable.

President Marcelo Rebelo de Sousa played a pivotal role in the lead-up to the election. Following Costa's resignation, he faced the critical decision of whether to allow the PS to nominate a successor or dissolve parliament and call for early elections. The President engaged in a series of consultations with party leaders and the Council of State and ultimately opted for early elections, reasoning that the government had lost public trust and a fresh mandate was necessary to restore confidence in the political system. This decision set the stage for a fiercely contested election and forced all the political parties to organise their campaigns and prepare for the electorate rapidly. The President's decision was seen by many as necessary to clear the air of suspicion and start anew.

The PS leadership contest that followed Costa's resignation became a key factor in the lead up to the election. The contest pitted two prominent figures, José Luís Carneiro and Pedro Nuno Santos, against each other, revealing the ideological divisions within the party. Carneiro, seen as a moderate, campaigned on a platform of stability and continuity, emphasising his electability. Santos, a champion of the left, advocated for a more progressive agenda. Santos ultimately won this contest, signalling a shift within the PS. This leadership change was critical because it had a direct impact on the party's overall electoral strategy, and public perception of the party's direction.

The PSD, led by Luís Montenegro, sought to capitalise on the PS's disarray. Montenegro's strategy focused on uniting the centre-right and curbing the influence of the far-right Chega party. This led to the formation of the AD, a coalition with the PP, positioned as a "reformist and moderate" force. The creation of this alliance was a calculated move to consolidate the right-wing vote and present a credible challenge to the PS. However, it also drew criticism from those who saw it as a means of legitimising Chega.

The formation of the AD coalition significantly impacted the electoral dynamics, presenting a clear alternative to the PS and increasing the pressure on the ruling party to regain public trust. While Montenegro ruled out any pre-election agreements with Chega, this strategy was seen by some as disingenuous, since Chega's support may have been required to form a government if the PSD/AD were unable to secure a majority.

During this period, Chega continued its ascent in Portuguese politics under the leadership of André Ventura. The party capitalised on public discontent, particularly regarding issues such as immigration and the perceived inadequacies of the traditional political establishment. Ventura's rhetoric was often divisive, but his message resonated with a segment of the population that felt ignored by the mainstream parties. Chega's growing popularity posed a challenge for the PS and the PSD, as they tried to navigate the complexities of a shifting political landscape. Chega consistently presented itself as a party willing to challenge the status quo and offered voters frustrated with the mainstream parties an alternative. Chega remained a key factor in the electoral calculation, with both the PS and PSD having to factor their likely level of support into their election strategies.

The economic context also played a significant role in the lead-up to the election. The country was grappling with several economic challenges, including rising inflation, the cost-of-living crisis, and concerns about the impact of the European Central Bank's monetary policy. The government's handling of these issues, particularly the controversial 2024 state budget, which included a hike in road tax for older vehicles, sparked widespread public anger. The economic situation contributed to a general sense of unease and provided ammunition for the opposition parties to attack the government's record. The public's economic anxieties and perceptions about how well the government handled them became key to voting intentions.

The ongoing crisis within the SNS (National Health Service) further exacerbated the situation. The shortage of doctors, the closures of A&E departments, and the cancellation of operations created an atmosphere of fear and disillusionment. The crisis was not simply a matter of logistics; it spoke to deeper systemic problems and revealed the government's inability to manage its key public services. The SNS crisis became a focal point for opposition attacks, with parties across the political spectrum criticising the government's handling of the situation, and calling for increased investment and better working conditions for healthcare professionals.

In addition to these major issues, two other controversies made headlines in the lead up to the early election: the Lisbon airport project and allegations of presidential favouritism. The choice of Alcochete as the preferred site for the new airport sparked immediate political disagreement, with the PSD forming a working group to re-evaluate the proposal, effectively delaying any final decision. This delay was criticised by the PS who called for swift action, and the situation demonstrated the difficulty of reaching consensus on major infrastructure projects. Furthermore, allegations surfaced that President Marcelo Rebelo de Sousa had used his influence to secure costly medical treatment for twin girls, which led to calls for a parliamentary hearing. These controversies, while not as seismic as the corruption scandal or the health crisis, added to the sense of unease, and public questioning of the government's competency and ethical standards.

The pre-election campaign was characterised by increasingly sharp exchanges between the main parties, with the PS, now under the leadership of Pedro Nuno Santos, attempting to distance itself from the corruption scandal and emphasise its commitment to social welfare. The PSD, on the other hand, sought to portray itself as the party of change and stability, capitalising on the public's disillusionment with the PS. Chega continued to disrupt the political landscape, using its now well established populists and provocative style to appeal to voters disillusioned with the mainstream parties.

Opinion polls conducted throughout this period showed a dynamic and unpredictable race, with both the PS and the PSD vying for public support. While the PS maintained a narrow lead in some polls, Chega continued to consolidate its position as the third most popular party. Public confidence in both Santos and Montenegro remained low, highlighting the challenges confronting both leaders as they geared up for the March elections.

The period leading up to the 10 March 2024 election was a turbulent and consequential one. The Operation Influencer scandal and its impact on the PS government, coupled with a series of other challenges including a healthcare crisis and an ongoing cost of living crisis, created a climate of uncertainty and heightened the stakes for all parties involved. The various political parties fought hard for electoral advantage, and the public was left to decide which vision for Portugal best served their interests. The early election was far more than just a change of government; it represented a fundamental test of the Portuguese political system and its ability to maintain public trust and address the pressing needs of its citizens. The outcome of the election was set to have a significant impact on the future of Portuguese democracy.

Operation Influencer

Operation Influencer, the corruption investigation that led to the dramatic resignation of Prime Minister Costa in November, was a seismic event that shook the foundations of Portuguese politics and cast a shadow over the country's political landscape.

The scandal, which involved allegations of bribery and influence peddling in the awarding of government contracts, not only triggered a political crisis but also exposed deep-seated concerns about transparency, accountability and the integrity of the political system.

The investigation unfolded against a backdrop of economic anxieties and a growing public disillusionment with the traditional political establishment, further amplifying its impact and raising profound questions about the direction of the country.

The investigation, known as Operation Influencer, centred on suspicions that government officials and other key figures had been involved in illicit activities related to the awarding of contracts for several major projects. These included, most notably, the exploitation of lithium mines, the development of a hydrogen power plant and the construction of a data centre. These were all projects that were important to the country's infrastructure and economic development plans, and the alleged corruption surrounding these projects raised serious questions about the government's competency and ethical standards. The very fact that the investigation focused on significant projects of national importance underscored the gravity of the allegations and their potential impact on the country's future.

The allegations suggested a pattern of bribery and influence peddling, with the investigation uncovering a network of individuals who had allegedly used their positions of power to secure contracts for their own benefit or for the benefit of associated parties. The scandal wasn't just about isolated incidents of corruption; it was about a system where undue influence and illicit practices had become normalised. This alleged normalisation of corruption was arguably one of the most damaging aspects of the scandal, as it fuelled public cynicism and eroded trust in those in power.

The investigation implicated several high-profile figures, including Prime Minister Costa's Chief of Staff, Vítor Escária, and Diogo Lacerda Machado, a lawyer allegedly close to Costa. The involvement of these figures, who were close confidants of the Prime Minister, raised questions about the extent of Costa's knowledge of, or involvement in, the alleged illicit activities. The fact that a significant corruption investigation reached the Prime Minister's inner circle had a devastating impact on his reputation and the credibility of his government.

Search warrants were executed at the Prime Minister's official residence, the PS headquarters and locations linked to the lithium and hydrogen projects. These searches, which uncovered evidence of "high-value meals and suspicious meetings", were a key aspect of the investigation and provided a glimpse into the alleged activities of those implicated. The searches, combined with the revelation of court-authorised taps on Costa's phone, suggested that investigators were taking the allegations seriously, and gathering strong evidence that those in power had abused their positions for their personal gain.

The taps on Costa's phone revealed conversations between the Prime Minister and key figures involved in the investigation. These conversations reportedly included discussions about environmental licensing for the lithium mines and conversations with Infrastructure Minister Galamba, who was already a defendant in the case. These revelations suggested the Prime Minister had direct contact with individuals implicated in the alleged illicit activities and that he was aware of the ongoing discussions and processes related to the contracts. The phone taps also led to a raid on Escária's office, where investigators seized a considerable amount of cash, further cementing suspicions of wrongdoing.

Prime Minister Costa, while denying any wrongdoing, ultimately chose to resign on 8 November 2023, stating that the "incompatibility between the dignity of his office and any suspicion of wrongdoing" made his position untenable. This resignation was a dramatic turning point in the investigation and had a major impact on the political landscape, plunging the country into a period of uncertainty and instability. Costa's decision to resign, rather than fight the allegations, was seen by some as an implicit admission of guilt or at least an awareness of the seriousness of the charges. It also led to the collapse of his government.

Operation Influencer's impact on public perception of the government was profound. It fuelled a sense of disillusionment and eroded trust in political institutions, making it harder for any political party to gain public confidence. The scale of the investigation and the involvement of individuals so close to the Prime Minister made it difficult for the public to see the government as anything other than corrupt and self-serving.

The opposition parties were quick to seize upon the crisis and called for President Rebelo de Sousa to dissolve parliament and call early elections. They argued that the government had lost its legitimacy and that new elections were necessary to restore public trust. The calls for elections were particularly forceful from the PSD, which saw a chance to capitalise on the PS government's collapse.

President Rebelo de Sousa's decision to call early elections on 10 March 2024, rather than allow the PS to nominate a successor, marked a turning point in Portuguese politics, ushering in a period of uncertainty and setting the stage for a potentially transformative general election. The President's decision was widely seen as a recognition of the government's failure and an understanding of the need for a fresh start for the country.

The resignation of Costa also triggered a leadership contest within the PS, further adding to the political turmoil. The contest, which pitted José Luís Carneiro against Pedro Nuno Santos, exposed divisions within the PS and revealed the different ideological factions fighting to control the party. Santos' victory in this leadership contest signalled a shift within the PS, with younger party members ascending to positions of influence. The leadership contest was more than just an internal party matter: it was seen as a reflection of the broader political challenges facing the country and the different paths that the PS could choose to take.

The PSD, led by Luís Montenegro, sought to capitalise on the PS's disarray and the public's disillusionment with the government, seeing it as an opportunity to gain power. Montenegro, in an attempt to appeal to more moderate voters, ruled out any pre-election agreements with Chega. However, this strategy was also met with suspicion, with many questioning whether Montenegro would be willing to work with Chega after the election if it proved necessary to form a government.

Operation Influencer unfolded amidst a backdrop of a healthcare crisis and ongoing concerns about the cost of living, with a 2023 report showing that a quarter of the population had struggled to pay for basic necessities that year. These challenges, exacerbated by the corruption scandal, created an atmosphere of unease and heightened public dissatisfaction with the government. The public's increasing anxieties about the economy and healthcare meant the corruption scandal was not just a political matter but a deeply personal one for many voters.

The sale of the power solutions company Efacec became a symbol of the government's perceived incompetence and lack of transparency. The fact that the company was sold for a fraction of the money the government had invested in it further fuelled public discontent and eroded trust in the government's ability to manage public assets.

The Lisbon airport project and allegations of presidential favouritism further added to the sense of unease. These additional controversies, while not directly related to Operation Influencer, contributed to the overall perception of a political system plagued by corruption and a lack of accountability. These smaller controversies meant that the public, and the opposition, had additional points to use to attack the government's ethical and moral standards, making it more challenging for any political party to gain public confidence.

The impact of Operation Influencer was not limited to the immediate political fallout. The scandal also raised serious questions about the role of the media and the judiciary in holding those in power to account, and the need for greater transparency and accountability in government contracts and procurement processes. The scandal also highlighted the potential for corruption to undermine democratic institutions and erode public trust in the political system.

In conclusion, Operation Influencer was far more than just a corruption investigation: it was a catalyst for significant political change and highlighted fundamental issues within the Portuguese political system. The scandal exposed deep-seated concerns about corruption and a lack of accountability, severely damaged public trust in the government and set the stage for the early general elections of 2024. The events surrounding Operation Influencer demonstrated the inherent fragility of democratic institutions and the very real need for constant vigilance, scrutiny and the promotion of ethical standards in public life. The scandal also highlighted the very real risks that corruption poses to a country's economic and social well-being, and the need for ongoing vigilance in protecting a nation's democratic values.

Index

www.ingramcontent.com/pod-product-compliance
Lightning Source LLC
Chambersburg PA
CBHW071013250726
48653CB00005B/1604